MENTAL MOUNTAINS
A FOUR AND A HALF YEAR JIGSAW PUZZLE

BY EMA DANTAS

Copyright © 2023 Ema de Jesus Joao Bras Dantas

All rights reserved.

No part of this book may be reproduced or utilized in any form or by any means, electronic or mechanical, including photocopying, recording, or by any information storage and retrieval system, without permission in writing from the author.

ISBN 978-0-9920506-1-0

In memory of my mom, Adelaide.

To my beautiful daughters, Patricia and Nicole. I am eternally grateful for your support and understanding when I lacked patience and didn't always focus on "being a mom" during the last decade of my life. Thank you for loving me and supporting me, faithfully. Patricia, thank you for picking up all the slack at LMP. Nicole, thank you for being my publicist and confidant. I love you both so much. There are no words that can faithfully convey it. God really blessed me with both of you.

*Ethan, Julia, thank you for being Vovo's happy pills.
I love you both so much.*

*To my two sons-in-law Dustin and Nico,
thank you for loving my daughters and cheerleading me.*

To Emmanuel Monssen, thank you for challenging me, and believing in me. Thank you for teaching me I could be stronger; and a better woman and mother. Thank you for always knowing when I needed a text message, and for being my best friend. And of course, thank you for that first glass of Stoneleigh Sauvignon Blanc.

CONTENTS

1. Why Climb Mountains..........................1
2. Adelaide..5
3. Introduction to Mountaineering............15
4. Peaks for Change Foundation..............19
5. Carstensz Pyramid...........................21
6. Altitude Sickness............................37
7. Kilimanjaro...................................43
8. Elbrus...51
9. Vinson Massif................................61
10. Aconcagua..................................73
11. Denali.......................................81
12. Kosciuszko (Kosi).........................93
13. Mind Over Mountain......................95
14. Everest 2021..............................99
15. Everest, Take Two.......................105
What's Next....................................119

PREFACE

When I saw the post office clerk pull out the envelope, I knew.

It took a lot to keep my composure and not start crying, but I managed to make it to the car, and then my tears just rolled down overpoweringly.

I didn't understand why I was crying. I had a certificate for each of the other mountains I climbed, but maybe because this one had official stamps. This one came to me by registered mail.

This one was confirmation that I climbed to the top of Everest and made it back safely. This one was confirmation that even though I may have felt somewhat a lack of the 'wow' factor for reaching the top, it represented that despite so much going on in my life during these last four and a half years, I made it.

I cried because the mountains ironically saved my life.

I cried because I realized: now what?

I cried because climbing the 7 summits did not raise the money we had wanted for Peaks for Change Foundation, for the 7 Summits for Mental Health campaign, benefiting the Center for Addiction and Mental Health (CAMH). However the mountains taught me so much about myself, about my personal mental health, about my resilience. They taught me importance of mental health and the importance of continuing to be an advocate.

Personally, I cried because during this period, my marriage ended, I lost Daisy my 15-year old Jack Russell; I had to sell my home and move. During this period I learned to depend on myself and trust myself.

The tears were also happy tears. I became the first Portuguese person to climb the 7 Summits, both versions. I learned to love mountains and learned to love myself, believe in myself and learned to trust Jesus.

CHAPTER 1
WHY CLIMB MOUNTAINS

It always come down to the question of "Why?".

When I was climbing, people kept asking me why? What made me climb mountains.

There are so many answers to this question. To be honest, when I started climbing, I really hadn't thought about why I was climbing. I just felt compelled to do it. It was a challenge that I knew was going to keep my mind occupied and therefore help my sanity.

A couple of weeks after I came back from climbing and successfully summiting Carstensz Pyramid, I wrote a thank you letter to my guide Emmanuel that gave a pretty good answer to the question of why. I said to him, "... or at least have the opportunity to do great things in this world and help others and not just be average. I never considered myself average. I don't want to be average."

When I started to climb, I didn't have a clear idea of why I had set my mind on climbing the 7 summits. Sure, I had an elevator pitch of why I was climbing. It was to raise awareness for mental health and raise funds for Peaks for Change Foundation's initiative "7 Summits for Mental Health". The initiative was in support of the Bridging Clinic for the Center of Addiction and Mental Health, in Toronto. I'll talk more about this later, however deep in my soul I had another reason for climbing.

The main reason I decided to climb mountains goes back to that one day when a severe migraine brought me home from the office. On that day I found a computer left on with an unlocked screen, and I stumbled on an inbox with over 2000 emails that drove home the devastating realization that the last decade of my life had been a lie. On that day in April 2009, I broke. I cried on my bedroom floor in the fetal position having just discovered my then husband had been cheating on me. He had slept with at least fourteen women.

After this, the next few months I recall being in a haze. Between fits of uncontrollable tears that would just flood my face, without warning, and a constant head fog, I had these moments in time I just wanted to know every detail of his betrayal. What was keeping me breathing was the 12 year old, only child in me; the one that wanted to be a detective. Back when I was twelve I had read all the Trixie Belden stories written by Julie Campbell. I read the translated Portuguese version, where the series were re-titled as "Patricia".

Beatrix "Trixie" Belden was a young teen that lived on her family farm, in the Hudson Valley area of New York. The first book, The Secret of the Mansion, established her friendship with a lonely, sheltered rich girl, Honey Wheeler, whose family had just moved into the Manor House next door. Trixie and Honey became friends and this book was about the girls' first case. I was hooked, all the way to adulthood, I believed I could be a good detective, and find all the answers.

I soon discovered that the haziness in my brain was because my soul was littered with broken pieces of my heart. I needed to put those pieces back together. Climbing mountains promised gusts of air, that would dissipate the fog in my head.

I have come to believe wholeheartedly that God gave us life to succeed, be happy and experience abundance and joy. Jesus walked the Earth and was not afraid to speak his mind, to be kind and to stand up for himself even though it raised a few eyebrows. I came to believe that the least I could do, in order to honour life, was to try and do everything I could to be joyful, kind and successful, even if I got stuck in the mud sometimes.

Being an entrepreneur means you cannot wallow in self-pity. You have to get up each day and just keep going. In my case, at this point and time in my life, continuing to work and build my company, kept me moving. One day at time. One client at a time, one win at a time, and one lesson at a time. Now I look back and find the similarities with climbing mountains - metaphorically. One Step at a Time.

Creating *Peaks for Change Foundation* was an extension of being an entrepreneur. This was more than a foundation; it was a way to give back. Our first initiative "Seven Summits for Mental Health" brought together my desire to end the stigma surrounding mental health and my desire to climb mountains.

Climbing a mountain, building Peaks and running a business all required hard work. Like a marriage, if you want to have great sex and a wonderful relationship, but you're not willing to work through some arguments and hard conversations, or make compromises and get creative, you will plateau and have nowhere to go. I wasn't going to let the breakdown of my marriage strand me with nowhere to go.

But how does this all relate to the question of why? Why mountains? Why climb for mental health?

You see, my mother was mentally ill. I cannot tell you her exact diagnosis, because a concrete one was never officially made by her various doctors. I know she was depressed. I have memories of her lying on the couch for days, looking as emotionally flat as her body. I now realize she was either bi-polar or schizophrenic. Or both.

The truth is, I was ashamed of her. I had no understanding of the personal internal war she was fighting nor did I have the tolerance or time to try to understand her. I lacked the ability to show her compassion and love.

I know I can't dwell in the past. I know I can't turn back the clock; life is not a Hollywood movie. But I can help others learn from my mistakes. I can be less tolerant of those speaking poorly about someone suffering with mental illness, whatever form it takes, and I can speak out and help end of the stigma surrounding mental health.

My mom's name was Adelaide. She was once a strong woman. I did love her. I just never told her. So now I climb mountains, in her honour and in mine.

CHAPTER 2
ADELAIDE

The struggle to understand mental health illness.

Unfortunately, my mother suffered from a mental illness that was never diagnosed or labeled, and this made it difficult for her.

Through the greater part of my adult life my relationship with my mother was one of turmoil, hate many times, harsh words, sadness, regret, heart break and anger mixed in with a yearning to be loved, accepted and happy.

My parents retired to Portugal in 1983 and my mother's symptoms and troubled behaviour started shortly thereafter.

Mental health issues and acceptance in Portugal, as in many other parts of the world including here at home in Canada, is still taboo in everyday life, regardless of how fashionable it is to "talk" about it in social media. When you combine that with spousal abuse, you have a lethal combination.

My mother was 68-years old at the time of her death. She was residing in a nursing home at the time. There, she was spoon fed pureed food. She was bathed and she wore diapers. She was restrained when sitting because she could not walk on her own, and when she tried, she would fall.

On January 6, 2013 her heart gave out and she died in the ambulance on the way from the nursing home to the local hospital. I believe she died of a broken heart. A broken heart that could not endure any more emotional trauma.

The last time I visited my mother at the nursing home was in September of 2012, and only for a few hours. I feel ashamed that it was only a few hours. At the time, I felt it was all I could manage. Today, as I look back, I feel regret. In hindsight, my feelings were petty and even a little ridiculous.

I had a lot of baggage where my parents were concerned; especially with my mother. It goes back to when I was five years old and my parents immigrated to Canada. Back then we lived in a shared home with an acquaintance from Portugal. At the time, my parents rented a one room flat, in a three floor home on Queen Street. We had a shared entrance and family room, and my parents had the only bedroom. I had to share a bed with the owner's older daughter, downstairs.

I remember one night I wet the bed and my parents argued. My mom defend me but my father kicked me so hard I fell and tumbled down the stairs to the bottom. I don't remember what happened after that, but I do recall being shipped back to Portugal to live with my paternal grandparents shortly thereafter. I didn't mind really because they were very caring. They showed me nothing but love until the day they died.

While living at my grandparents, I remember feeling mad at my mother but not my father. Even when my parents came to visit around Christmas, I didn't want to hug her. I wasn't excited to see her, nor did I run to her when they arrived. I just remember staying seated by the fire in my grandparents' kitchen and feeling afraid. Afraid that I had to go with my parents. I can still hear my mother's voice and her telling me she missed me. I recall her giving me a Timex watch and trying to get me, her own child, to smile or talk to her.

Now I realize that must have broken her heart but at the time, I remember feeling nothing for them.

This set the stage for my relationship with my parents. I left home at the age of 17, got married and had a baby shortly after I turned 18.

As an adult, I blamed my mother for not leaving my father. I felt superior to her as I rationalized that I would never have chosen my husband over my child. I judged her, and in retrospect, probably contributed to her unhappy life. To this day, it's a realization I live with.

We have all read and heard about the effects of spousal abuse. In Canada we are fortunate to be able to call the police for help, lay charges and file for restraining orders. In Portugal, this finally became possible in 2010 but for years, my mother's cry for help fell on deaf ears. The local Police (National Republic Police also known as GNR) and the local hospital did nothing to help her.

I remember one time my parents called me in Canada. It was the middle of the night when they called. My mom had walked out of the house after my dad had beaten her. My dad had enlisted the help of the local police. They found her and brought her home. During the call I asked to speak with one of the officers that was still at the house, and when he came on the phone, I said he needed to take my dad into custody. I told him that as soon as the officers left, my dad would beat my mom again. What this officer said next will forever be engraved in my memory and haunt me for the rest of my life:

"What kind of daughter wants to have her father arrested?" he said to me.

"The kind that wants to see both parents alive," I answered choked up.

"Your mother is crazy and a man can only take so much," he answered and hung up.

I was angry. The officer made it clear he wasn't going to help my mom so I wrote an email to the local police station and reported the incident. My dad was brought in for questioning and released. All this accomplished was my dad being furious with me.

On another occasion shortly after, my parents called again in the middle of the night and all I could hear was my mother screaming, "Ema, he is going to kill me, Ema, dad is going to kill me honey." And it was followed by my dad screaming at her, telling her to be quiet. I would just cry on my end of the telephone, an ocean away.

My mother started going in and out of psychiatry hospitals for treatment shortly after my parents moved to Portugal in 1983. She spent months at a time in a private mental health facility, "Casa de Saude Rainha Santa Isabel" near Coimbra. She would stay there about three months at a time, then function for about a year, then go back and so forth.

For approximately twelve years she stop going into the psychiatric treatment facilities and auto medicated herself, often overmedicating because she would visit every doctor possible in Portugal and even in Spain. With no regulations in place and a medical system that encompassed both public and private doctors, it was and continues to be pretty easy to get any drug you want.

Portugal is on Western European time, meaning they are five hours ahead of me here in Toronto, Canada. The last three years of my mother's life and whenever my parents had a fight, they would call me in the middle of the night my time. They would have been fighting all night and by early morning it was at its peak. When they called, I would hear them screaming at each other on the other side of the phone. One time, my mother was screaming and repeating, "He is going to kill me, he is going to kill me. Ema, please help, he is going to kill me".

These cries for help haunt me to this day.

Another time during a screaming match, the phone line died as I heard my dad hitting my mom. I kept trying to call back, but I was powerless thousands of miles away and worried about my mother. Finally, someone answered the phone and identified himself as an officer of the GNR. He was also my father's friend. He informed me everything was under control and that the police had been called to my parent's home by a neighbor. When I asked about my mother and he stated she was ok, and that my dad had just gotten upset and hit her but that he promised not to do it again. I told the officer my father need to be charged as this happened all the time. The officer's exact response was:

"You are a bitch of a daughter. You want us to arrest your father for giving your mom a little beating? What kind of daughter are you?"

I answered, again as I had the other time, "the kind that wants to see both parents alive, not have one kill the other. One of these days he is going to kill her."

The officer responded, "Well, he promised he will not hit her again. So, I am going to hang up." And he did.

This officer must have known I had filed a complaint the previous time. I found out later that he filed a report to document having been at their house.

After one of my mother's state hospital hospitalizations, the psychiatrist in charge informed me that my mother heard voices and needed to be on the proper medication to function. At the time, I didn't realize that was a symptom of schizophrenia, and honestly, I didn't take the time to learn more.

This doctor also suggested I ask the state to take custody of her care, as my father was not capable of effectively and safely taking care of her.

I followed this suggestion in 2006 and petitioned the courts to allow me to put my mom in a hospital. The court ruled that she did not seem to be a danger to herself or others, and that since the report from the local police stated she faced no harm from my dad, the court could not force her to go into a psychiatric facility for help, even though they realized problems existed.

From here the beatings continued. I am ashamed to say I stopped talking to my mom. Every time I tried talking to her, she would call me names and scream at me and say I did not care about her. My father would take the phone from her or would call me when she was asleep and tell me how sick she was. He kept telling me he could not take care of her. Time went by. In 2010, I hired a lawyer and tried once again to petition the courts. I wanted to get guardianship over their affairs so I could oversee their care. I wanted to be able to put both my parents in a retirement/nursing home, where my mom could receive counselling and most importantly, where they would not be in a position to hurt each other. Somewhere my father would not be able to beat her.

This caused even more anger from my mother. She interpreted this action as me wanting to steal from them. When my father would call, she would again be screaming in the background, calling me derogatory names and making accusations against me.

My dad hired his usual local lawyer, but when it seemed the court would rule in my favour, he fired him and brought in an out-of-area lawyer, to whom he provided a skewed version of their lives and mine. My father paid "witnesses" that had never met me, to say how awful I was and how I did not care for them. As hard as my lawyer tried to rebuff this, in the end, the judge's hands were tied by the law. My father was able to prove he could recognize money, do basic math tests, knew what day of the week it was, where he was, etc. and claimed he could take care of my mother. My case was denied.

Approximately two weeks after that final court decision, I called my lawyer requesting he go to the local hospital to determine why a nurse there said she could not update me on my mother's situation and had instructed me to call back and speak with a social worker.

My lawyer said he would make a few calls right away and then added:

"… this is a huge coincidence, just a few days ago I saw the judge that ruled on our case and he apologized for not being able to go in our favour, He said all the witnesses presented stated your father was capable of taking care of your mother, and that was what the law required. The tests about him being able to count money and being able to understand paying bills and so forth, left his hands tied. I did tell him this will not be the last we hear from this couple. Let's hope there is not a tragedy soon".

Well, there was.

I will never know if it was the court case that contributed to the increased beatings my father inflicted on my mother but he rendered her brain damaged. I will never know if I made matters worse trying to shelter her. Rationally I realize my father's behaviour had nothing to do with me or anything I did or did not do, but the emotional side of me will always question my actions.

Research on domestic violence in Europe indicates that every day one in five women is a victim of domestic abuse.

According to information found on the website Stop Violence Against Women, A Project of the Advocates of Human Rights, "worldwide, 40-70% of all female murder victims are killed by an intimate partner."

The same source states, "Statistics on the prevalence of the problem indicate that domestic violence is a worldwide epidemic."

The Canadian Women's Foundation fact sheet "Moving Women out of Violence" states, "On average, every six days a woman in Canada is killed by her intimate partner. In 2009, 67 women were murdered by a current or former spouse or boyfriend."

An article in CNN.com, written by Amanda MacMillan from Health.com, August 2, 2011 reads, "Women are drastically more likely to develop a mental disorder at some point in their lives if they have been the victim of rape, sexual assault, stalking, or intimate-partner violence, according to a new study in the Journal of the American Medical Association."

In her article, Amanda quotes Andrea Gielen and states, "While connection between these harrowing experiences and poor mental health is hardly surprising, experts say the new findings highlight just how strongly the two problems are intertwined – and how important it is for doctors and other health-care workers to ask women about past episodes of violence, even if they happened years ago.

When professionals are treating women with depression or mental issues, it's best to be clued into the fact that violence might be behind it," says Andrea Gielen, Sc.D., director for the Center for Injury Research and Policy at Johns Hopkins University, in Baltimore, who was not involved in the study.

Amanda also added:

"Researchers in Australia analyzed health data from a nationally representative sample of Australian women between the ages of 16 and 85. Episodes of sexual assault, stalking, and other "gender-based violence" were all too common, with 27% of the group reporting at least one episode of abuse.

Fifty-seven percent of the women with a history of abuse also had a history of depression, bipolar disorder, post-traumatic stress, substance abuse, or anxiety (including panic disorder and obsessive-compulsive disorder), versus 28% of the women who had not experienced gender based violence.

Among women who had been exposed to at least three types of violence, the rate of mental disorders or substance abuse rose 89%."

The article concludes with a quote from Susan Rees:

"The extent and strength of the association we found was surprising and very concerning," says lead author Susan Rees, PhD., a senior research fellow in psychiatry at the University of New South Wales, in Sydney.

Rees and her colleagues can't say for sure the mental health problems in the study were triggered by the violence, or whether women with the preexisting mental health issues were more likely to experience violence. (They did, however, control for a range of potential mitigating factors, including socioeconomic status and a family history of psychiatric problems.)

But there is "ample evidence" that traumatic events – especially interpersonal traumatic events, such as domestic abuse – can trigger mental problems, Rees says.

Moreover, she adds, "episodes of gender-based violence often occur very early in life, whereas mental disorders often don't surface until years later."

I know my children will never know the other side of my mother. She was a strong, hard working woman.

For example, when we first moved to Canada, my mother worked on a farm in the Chatham area during the summers, picking cucumbers and tomatoes. This was usually about two months of work. During the spring months, the rest of summer and into fall, she worked at night picking worms in parks and golf courses. Like many Portuguese immigrants in the seventies and even into the eighties, these were the types of jobs available.

I have great childhood memories of me going to the farm with my mother. I ate my first peanut butter and jam sandwich at the farm owned by the Cameron family. It was rainy that day so we ate inside the home with Mr. Cameron, his wife and young son, Patrick who was my age. It was memorable because it was not typical Portuguese food.

I also have memories of my mother working in a shoe factory, in Toronto on College Street, directly across from my school St. Helens. I remember she would see me playing at recess and see me going outside very early during lunch. In those days I did not like my lunch so I would toss it in the garbage. She knew I did that and always called me out about it when I got home. She was also a cool mom. She bought me my first tube top. She shaped my eyebrows with tweezers for the first time and put light blush on my cheeks.

But those aren't the memories that stand out for me. The abuse at the hands of my father are what I remember the most.

My dad not only physically abused my mom, he did so emotionally as well. My mom stood by him, even after several reported affairs and after he was arrested for indecent public exposure and sentenced to six months in a Portuguese prison.

This was all very traumatic for me as a young teenager however I can now recognize, that as a grown woman, it must have been devastating for my mother. I believe this emotional abuse broke her heart and shattered her self-confidence.

As a teenager, I thought my mom had just become a mean person. Today, regrettably a late realization on my part, I realize she was struggling to cope. The pain of betrayal from a spouse can be unbearable, even difficult to recover from. Looking back now, in my opinion, it was the beginning of the end of her life.

I will be eternally sorry that I left her alone in her journey. I stigmatized my mother because she was mentally ill. I judged her.

I feel guilt and regret that I treated my mom unfairly. In my shame of her and my selfishness, I deprived her of knowing her own grandchildren and also great-grandchildren.

If I had understood sooner and not felt so uncomfortable around her and my dad, perhaps she would not have felt so alone. Perhaps she would have realized that she was loved.

I had many opportunities to spend time with my mom. In September 2012, I visited her in the nursing home but chose not to spend the entire day with her, even though I could have. At that point she couldn't talk to me but I know I could have simply kept her company. I could have hugged her. I could have held her hand and shown her pictures of her grandchildren. I could have told her all about them but I didn't.

I knew she could still hear me but I was so uncomfortable being there, seeing her being fed and her eating like she was famished. I desperately wanted to distance myself. I was embarrassed. There were other times too that I could have been more compassionate towards my mom. Times I could have acknowledged her cry for help. Times like when I went back to Portugal to attend my godmother's funeral, and barely made time to visit her. Then, all I could think about was that my godmother had been killed in a deadly car accident while travelling from Lisbon to northern Portugal to spend time with my grandparents. It was reported they had tried to pass a car and a truck hit them head on, taking the lives of my godmother, her son, husband

and her husband's niece who was travelling with them to reunite with her family, after having spent holidays with her aunt and uncle.

I had gone to Portugal with my youngest daughter, who was eleven months old at the time, and I remember my mom held out her arms to her and said, "Is this our little girl?". She held her with love.

But later when I cried at the loss of my godmother, my mother blurted out, "you are sad for Godmother and crying; you will not cry for me when I die".

Her saying this made me angry. I found it so selfish and inappropriate but reflecting today, I see it as her being needy, sad and confused. Instead of anger, I could have responded with love and said, "of course I will cry mom, I love you too".

Now I cry for my mom. I loved her and I miss her.

Perhaps she felt the same love looking into my daughter's eyes as I do when I look into my grandchildren's eyes. Perhaps she felt that same love, as I feel for mine.

I really never gave her the chance. A couple of days later, I left and took my child with me to my in-laws at the time. Instead of spending more time with my mom, I always felt the need to be far away from her.

There were many other times. Too many to list. Suffice it to say I always felt like a stranger near my parents. Now I look back with regret, because even as a stranger, my mom was a human being, she was mentally ill and she deserved my compassion and care. I feel I failed her.

When I went to Portugal to see my grandfather who was on his death bed, slowly losing his battle with cancer and nearing his end, my mother was being hospitalized for her illness. I remember walking into the hospital room where my mom was and her being so happy to see me that she said out loud, "my daughter", and hugged me so tight I thought she would never let go. I felt uncomfortable and shame. I wanted to run away. It must have hurt her deeply when I said I was there because her father-in-law was dying and I came to say goodbye.

My mom was mentally ill and I was ashamed of her. I had no patience or tolerance.

I know I cannot dwell in the past. I can't turn back the clock. However, I am hoping that someone can learn from my mistakes.

Today, I have less patience for people that speak ill of mentally ill persons.

When I told my aunt, my father's sister, that my mom was in the hospital and would not be going back home as my father was being charged for hitting her, I remember her exact words, "Oh... well I am sorry, she deserved it! Who can put up with that. I am sorry but she was a mean person."

These words hurt me deeply but instead of defending my mom, I simply got upset and then vented at home with my daughter and then husband.

No one deserves to be beaten. Certainly no one deserves to be beaten to the point of turning into a vegetable like my mom. She lost her ability to walk on her own, to feed herself and to go to the bathroom without help. She lost the ability to talk.

I thank God for his grace and kindness, and I actually thank my aunt's hurtful words for stirring the desire in me to see my mom before she passed.

Despite this understanding, I still feel hurt over all the pictures in my parents' home where my face had been careful cut out, however I no longer feel angry. I feel sad that my mom was unable to experience the love of her daughter, and sad she couldn't experience the joy of her grandchildren and great-grandchildren. I feel a responsibility for that.

Despite my upbringing, I have two daughters that are well balanced, caring young ladies whom I love very much. My older daughter now has two children of her own, who I also adore and soak up their hugs and kisses. I love the sweet sound of them calling me 'vovo'; it is just priceless.

When I look at these precious children I see beautiful blue eyes. Familiar eyes. My mother's eyes.

CHAPTER 3

INTRODUCTION TO MOUNTAINEERING

Dealing with my parent's mental health, and at the same time trying to navigate my personal life, in a marriage that was filled with mistrust, lies and adultery was suffocating. I couldn't function many days.

In 2010, I started running to raise money for ALS of Canada, because Charles Valliere, one of my company's French translators had been diagnosed with ALS.

Charles had only been employed with me at Language Marketplace for less than one year when he was diagnosed with ALS. It was through this hire, and subsequent events, that I believe God started to speak to me. Not literally of course, but through people and situations being put in my path to help me heal. My taking up running in support of ALS was the beginning; baby steps, but definitely the beginning.

My interest in running continued. I even started reading a running magazine, Running World. I remember that in 2015, an advertisement for training to climb Denali by RMI Expeditions caught my eye. It was an all-women, six day Denali Prep Course that was taking place on Mount Rainier, Washington. To be honest, I didn't even know where Denali was so I googled it. I remember sitting in the living room reading about the training on the company's page and feeling an urge to climb mountains. Actually, I was feeling the urge to run, or walk, or get away from the pain I was feeling. I didn't sign up but I did save this magazine issue. It sat and became part of my decor for a couple years.

Eventually Charles died, and it reminded me of my mom who had died in 2013. I was struggling in my life personally and desperately trying to find a way to heal. To survive.

So, in early 2017, I signed up to climb Rainier and do the Denali Prep course. I had high expectations of what this course would be and how good it would be for my soul. I was excited. I also knew that if I was going to climb Mount Rainier, that I would need to follow the pre-course training schedule by RMI Expeditions so I would be prepared for the experience.

When I got there, I quickly learned that I didn't train properly, but then I didn't really know any better.

Looking back through my diary, on May 8, 2017 I wrote:

> "I now train 7 days a week. I am training based on "Fit to Climb" by RMI, so I am ready for my upcoming Denali Prep course with RMI's Expedition Skills Seminar – Emmons, which is a six day instructional mountaineering course with a summit attempt on Mount Rainier via the Emma's Glacier route.
>
> At the same time, I am learning to rock climb and I have a personal trainer to help me build more of my upper body strength to tackle the Carstensz Pyramid (more on that later).
>
> Today, it was a particular tough day. I had hiked 3 hours yesterday as per this week's schedule from RMI's weekly program, and it was to be followed by 7 hours of hiking today, with a weighted backpack. I currently have 37 pounds on my pack.
>
> When you are running a marathon your mind plays games with you. At least mine does!!! First you are excited to start the race and usually about around 10 km you start regretting having signed up for the full marathon. Then just around the split, you are resigned to run the whole thing. And when you are on your last 4-5 km, you question your sanity.
>
> That was me today. At about 4 km away from home, and at about 6 hours of hiking time. I pondered using my cell phone and asking my family to come pick me up. I contemplated sitting and leaving my backpack on the side of the road and going later to pick it up. I worried about not being able to climb.
>
> Then I reach the steps of my side door and I knew that tomorrow morning I would lace up my running shoes and do the training session on the schedule. Because like running, hiking is peaceful, challenging and I am doing it because I enjoy it.
>
> Like when I was training for a marathon, I filled a bath and I let my body indulge for 20 minutes with the Jacuzzi jets at full capacity. I am aware this is a luxury that will not be available to me in my tent, but I am still home, so no harm in taking advantage of it!
>
> Training is hard physically, but also mentally. Today my brain was more tired than my body, and thus they fought."

Reflecting on this entry and how hard the training was, even at this stage, I also remember finding peace. Peace in the solitude, and peace in challenging myself. I had even decided to challenge myself further and committed to climbing 7 Summits for Mental Health for Peaks for Change Foundation and was preparing to climb Carstensz Pyramid not long after Mount Rainier.

But this peace was soon shattered, when I went to the Denali Prep course to train with a group of unknown women. My first climb, Mount Rainier was the most demoralizing experience.

Sure, I learned quite a bit, including things that may not stand out for some. I learned that I could sleep in a tent no matter the surface; snowy and icy surfaces or even on a dirt ground surface. I learned I could share a tent with two other women. While this may not seem like much, it was a great discovery and learning experience for me as I had never camped before.

I also learned that even though in the past I have enjoyed other "women only" learning environments, I did not enjoy this one as much. Perhaps it was because in the past I was only there to have fun, with other members of my gender, such as surfing in Costa Rica and Mexico. Or perhaps it was because some of my other experiences during the training felt wrong, like when I was carrying more than half my own body weight in my backpack as we climbed, while someone else in the group had their pack lightened to make their climb easier.

Perhaps my experience was impacted because I was too anxious to learn and at the same time, hurting from my recently broken ribs (more about that later on).

Whatever the reason, I was disappointed. I was disappointed in my own enthusiasm. I was disappointment in the lack of excitement and enthusiasm I expected to feel training with a large group of women. I kept looking for that "women power" I expected to feel. It just wasn't there.

When I trained at home or when I ran, I ran and trained alone. I spent months training for this first climb, but I did most of it alone. Now, in this group of women, I had to accommodate for the pace of others. Whether it was getting ready to go each day and having to wait for others that were slow to get going, or throughout the day as we continued our climb, at various paces, I found the journey tiring and un-motivating.

I felt a lack of trust with my fellow participants. I considered myself a self-reliant person who only gives trust once it has been earned, and now to be roped and connected with complete strangers, climbing a mountain, caused me anxiety.

As a group of women, learning to mountaineer, it felt more competitive than educational. It even felt unkind at times. This experience was not confidence building, on the contrary, it was discouraging.

Our guides, all women as well, were thoughtful wonderful people, but as teachers and guides, they were not motivating or encouraging. They failed to look at each one of us as pupils and instead treated us as competitors. They failed to see beyond our appearances and physical attributes. They perpetuated the stereotype of women competing with one another, incapable of working together to support each other in reaching a common goal. And I, eager to find my tribe of women, was discouraged.

Throughout the years that followed, at each summit I completed, I inevitably remembered how I almost gave them the power to crush my soul.

I often think that perhaps there was a greater lesson in my experience with this group. I am not talking about learning how to walk with crampons and tighten them properly (which

I did), or how to use my ice axe or even how to relieve myself while on a mountain (also did both), I am talking about how to trust in myself. Trust in my ability to climb. Trust in my ability to stay warm and know the protocols of the mountain to do my business in the wilderness (washroom). Trust that I was enough.

This all didn't occur for me until later. When I returned from my training on Mount Rainier in June 2017, and was asked how it went, I could only give a short answer. I could only say to my co-workers, family and friends, "My training session was ok."

Luckily for me, my friend Emmanuel probed deeper. I had expressed how much I hated climbing and that I couldn't do it.

After relating my experience, he simply assured me, "Don't worry. Climbing with a group made up with mostly men, is not like that. Carstensz will be different, you will see".

I trusted him.

I knew too that despite my experience during this training course that I still marveled at the beauty of the mountains, these majestic God created wonders. I was on my way to my first addiction - listening to the silence of nature up high in the mountains, admiring unobstructed views that extend for miles.

CHAPTER 4
PEAKS FOR CHANGE FOUNDATION

One of the defining moments of my friendship with Emmanuel, was when late one summer evening sitting in his backyard, he looked at me and said, "give me $100,000.00 and I can show you all the good that can be done in the world with it."

It was a general statement on a discussion we were having about charities and helping those in need around the world.

This brain storming session with Emmanuel sitting in lawn chairs, with the grass caressing our bare feet and drinking a glass of white wine, talking about all the things one can do brewed in my mind. This lead to my idea of founding a charitable foundation, to help end the stigma surrounding mental health. We knew that if just one person could feel like their life was worth living when they were feeling like no-one cared, then this charity, and our work would be worth it.

A couple weeks later I had messaged Emmanuel, "Peaks for Change". He had responded, "What is that?" "The name of the charity foundation I want to create," I wrote back.

"Ok," was his only response.

"And I am going to climb the 7 summits to bring awareness to mental health and donate the money to CAMH," I added on another text. CAMH is the Centre for Addiction and Mental Health located in Ontario.

Emmanuel was quick to remind me, "You can't climb, you are afraid of heights and you do know you need to sleep in a tent Ema. There are no bathrooms! No showers and did I mention, you are afraid of heights!"

I can't remember how long it took me to respond, but I know, I planted the idea that he would train me and he would climb with me, to teach me. And I promised to learn and work hard and to sleep in a tent.

Emmanuel is not a jump first, ask questions later kind of man, but he is a good friend. While I let the idea take root in his mind, I contacted CAMH and set a meeting with the CAMH Foundation where I proposed my idea of the charity and climbing mountains for mental health as our first initiative. My goal was to raise $700,000.00; $100,000.00 per mountain to all be donated to CAMH. They agreed.

I now see how naive I was but at the time, I didn't realize how difficult it would be to raise that much money in the name of mental health. My main experience was in raising money for ALS, which was very different. ALS is a rare disease. Mental health on the other hand affects approximately 1 in 4 Canadians, and is rarely talked about. And in my opinion, mental health scares people, even if they don't admit it.

During the "in-between time" from idea of the foundation to actual let's go do this stage, I had gone to an all-women's surf camp in Mexico. This camp was a completely different experience from the all-women Denali Prep course. It was amazing, inspiring and supportive. I left that camp believing I could surf the soup bowl in Hawaii!

I recall as if it was yesterday, walking while eating an ice-cream at the end of an afternoon, in the little fishing village Sayulita, as my cell phone rang. When I picked it up, Emmanuel simply said, "So you really want to climb?" I said smiling, "Yes."

"Fine. So, we start with Carstensz Pyramid in Indonesia. FX from Terra Ultima wants to go do an expedition there for the first time. It will be a great price and I will go as the Canadian guide and keep you safe." Emmanuel is always to the point.

"Ok. Thank you!" was all I could say as I tried my best to be nonchalant, as I was the happiest woman on planet earth at that moment. I still see myself sitting on a bench, chit chatting with a huge smile on my face. I was going to go climb. OMG, I was going to climb mountains!

They say you never forget when you fall in love for the first time. Well, it was at this very moment, on that day, with ice-cream in one hand and a cell phone in another, talking to my best friend on the other side of the phone line, that my stomach had butterflies and I knew I was going to fall in love with mountains.

When I broke the news about my idea for the foundation's first initiative to Steve (my husband at the time), we had a huge fight. Even though he was supportive in creating a charity, he was dead against it being for mental health. Even though he pretended to understand and support me about climbing mountains, like the rest of our relationship, it proved to be a farce.

But I was resolved. I put together a Board of Directors, mostly friends and family who supported me wholeheartedly. Emmanuel joined, and CAMH supported us in receiving donations.

While we waited for our charity status from the Canada Revenue Agency for Peaks for Change Foundation, I started training.

CHAPTER 5
CARSTENSZ PYRAMID

I became the first Portuguese woman to climb Carstensz Pyramid when I summited on October 11, 2017.

The journey to Carstensz Pyramid began on the evening of Wednesday, September 27, 2017. By the time I sat in the Toronto Air France / KLM Lounge I was a little calmer than I had been at home a few hours earlier. Even when I was arriving at the airport, I was having a mini nervous breakdown. My heart strings were stretched taut. I was feeling scared, guilty even, and yet deep down I was feeling a sense of excitement with the sense I knew this was what I had to do.

At heart, I am more of a home body. When I travel, I like hotel rooms with a nice bed, large bath, and of course a gorgeous view. In this case though, I was already looking forward to being back home with my family.

The day before I left, Paulo, one of my account coordinators at Language Marketplace, read me Psalm 91:

1. Whoever dwells in the shelter of the most high will rest in the shadow of the almighty.
2. I will say of the lord, "he is my refuge and my fortress, my god, in whom i trust."
3. Surely he will save you from the fowler's snare and from the deadly pestilence.
4. He will cover you with his feathers, and under his wings you will find refuge; his faithfulness will be your shield and rampart.
5. You will not fear the terror of night, the arrow that flies by day,
6. Nor the pestilence that stalks in the darkness, nor the plague that destroys at midday.
7. A thousand may fall at your side, ten thousand at your right hand, but it will not come near you.
8. You will only observe with your eyes and see the punishment of the wicked.
9. If you say, "the lord is my refuge," you make the most high your dwelling,
10. No harm will overtake you; no disaster will come near your tent.
11. For he will command his angels concerning you to guard you in all your ways;
12. They will lift you up in their hands, so that you will not strike your foot against a stone.

13. You will tread on the lion and the cobra; you will trample the great lion and the serpent.
14. "Because he loves me," says the lord, "I will rescue him; I will protect him, for he acknowledges my name.
15. He will call on me, and i will answer him; I will be with him in trouble, I will deliver him and honor him.
16. With long life I will satisfy him and show him my salvation."

He then graciously prayed and asked Jesus to keep me company during this journey. He also asked God to show me anything I have been too blind to see or find out about myself.

Throughout the coming four and a half year journey, God not only kept me safe, but led me in a path of personal healing and finding comfort in Jesus.

I reflected on this while waiting for my flight. I was on my way to climb my first of seven summits I had pledged to do on behalf of Peaks for Change Foundation. This summit would be the most technical one, and I was the only female in the group. I was nervous but relaxed when Emmanuel, my guide and best friend finally strolled in to catch the flight.

It was an 8 hour flight overnight to Amsterdam, Netherlands, with an almost 9 hour layover before our next flight. This gave us enough time to take the train from the airport to the center of the city. As we walked through customs before exiting the airport, the border officers rolled their eyes when we said we were going sightseeing.

Amsterdam is extremely clean, there are bicycles everywhere and even some dedicated bike lanes with stop lights. I had never been outside the Amsterdam airport, so I was happy to have enough time for the one hour canal cruise to see one of the cities named as one of the 100 most important places in the world!

In Amsterdam you can frequently smell pot in the street, and as we explored the city, we saw there were many cafes to smoke and buy pot. Our friend Adam, who was climbing with us and had been in Amsterdam a couple days ahead of us, texted Emmanuel a cafe to try. With our iPhones in hand, we followed the blue dot on our screen to go get ourselves a joint. We were in Amsterdam after all, and at the time, pot was still illegal in Canada.

Emmanuel, who had been there before, gave me a tour of the Red District. It was just like I had heard it described; prostitutes displaying themselves in windows looking for clients. It saddened me to see tourists walking past these windows, looking in with the same enthusiasm they had shown a few feet away looking at an old church and building.

As we continued to walk down the very narrow cobblestone street, we passed several sex toy stores. Emmanuel made a couple of joking comments that took me a bit to understand. Maybe I was being slow or naive, but I just attributed it to my brain being a bit sluggish after a few drags of the joint we had shared.

Emmanuel always sees the humour in life. He sees the cup half full and readily shares his viewpoints. For me, it was the first glimpse of understanding that life does not have to be black and white, we can add some colour to it.

Back at the airport, sitting in another KLM lounge and waiting to board our next fight, I gave thanks for the wonderful family, in particular my daughters and grandchildren, that Jesus had given me. I missed them already. I miss my husband Steve, who at that time, at least on the surface, was on my side and giving me his love, encouragement and full support.

We arrived in Bali, Indonesia on Saturday September 30, 2017. Indonesia is 12 hours ahead of Canada.

The volcano, Mount Agung had not erupted yet, but it was fuming in rage. The locals in Bali seemed unconcerned. Even though all news reports stated eruption was imminent, like everything, the volcano was in God's hands and timetable.

I remember that after our plane landed and as I waited for my two duffle bags, I felt relieved to be off the plane, stretching my legs and mind after the long journey. I was finally in Bali.

I was anxious watching the luggage carousel go round and round, waiting to see my duffle bags. These bags contained all my climbing supplies and I knew their contents were irreplaceable. This feeling would repeat itself every single climbing trip. Once I could see the familiar bags on the conveyor belt coming towards me, I was able to breathe a bit easier. Emmanuel's arrived as well.

Our hotel was only a few kilometres from the airport; however the journey took an hour. It seemed to take forever. Morning or evening rush hour traffic on Gardner Expressway in Toronto is a "speedway" compared to that drive!

We spent a couple days exploring Bali. I was disappointed. I had totally over fantasized Bali and blamed that on advertising. The hotel itself was accurate, but then the Four Seasons' chain tends not to disappoint, but I had visualized surfing, gorgeous beaches, and maybe even falling in love like Julia Roberts did in Eat, Pray, Love!

In reality, the beaches were empty, and the surfing schools and surfboard rental places were slightly deserted. I understood that Mount Agung was threatening to erupt, but our plane alone was packed with people, and the airport equally busy. I was at lost figuring out where all the tourists were. I quickly concluded that everyone was at their hotel pool because the beaches stunk. I mean they smelled bad! There was lots of plastic garbage being washed ashore, the water felt like a freight ship had leaked expired hair conditioner or suntan oil and smelled like dirty dish water. Not to mention, there were no waves. I was disappointed.

Despite this experience, my mind raced in anticipation of what was to come but I felt calm. I questioned if I really could be the first Portuguese woman to climb Carstensz Pyramid.

Bali was only a stopover on our travels to Timika, West Papua, to climb the long awaited Carstensz Pyramid. As the rest of our team trickled in, we did some sightseeing before taking a flight from Denpasar, Bali, to Timika, West Papua. Our flight left at 1:30 am local time and I was tired. I needed coffee!

As I prepared for the 4 hours plus of flying, sandwiched in the middle seat between Adam and Phillipe, two other team mates, I realized I had asked for a window seat. Unfortunately, this request fell on deaf ears. Welcome to Indonesia.

When we arrived at the Timika airport, our whole team was excited as we again watched the conveyor belt waiting for our duffle bags. We all looked like "hikers" with our backpacks, and as we waited, a few of our guys started a conversation with a handful of men that seemed to be from China.

"You guys climbing Carstensz?" Adam asked them.

They told us that yes, indeed they were. This was their 3rd try. And no, they would not be trekking in, as they had tried it once and aborted. Their group would be taking the helicopter. Secretly this answer scared us, well, maybe just me, and maybe just a little. I think we felt stronger and braver than them because we would be trekking in. I personally thought that they just wanted to brag that they had climbed Carstensz and the helicopter was just the easiest way to go. I was not fazed at what awaited us at that moment. Little did I know...

As we piled our duffle bags into pushcarts and headed to the exit, we were all stopped and our passports were taken away.

"What?!"

"Why?"

"What's going on?"

I felt completely powerless without my Canadian passport. We were left speechless.

Denny, our Indonesian head guide hired by Terra Ultima our Canadian expedition travel agent, was gone and I could see him outside looking at us trapped inside. I didn't understand what was going on or why he left us though he later claimed he left us on purpose, as a kind of test to see how we would handle ourselves when we encountered hostility towards us.

Thanks for the warning Denny!

Now that I have had time to think about it, and have the experience of seven other mountains, I don't believe Denny's reasoning. In the end, this trip left a lot to be desired in terms of organization. In my view and in retrospect, the real reason Denny left us was to see if he could save money and get away with not paying an official off.

From what I learned later, Indonesians, and particularly those from Papua, don't like tourists or foreigners. It was said that locals don't see the monetary benefit tourists bring in when they come to explore their country. Strange as it seems, it is like they believe we want to invade their country when in reality, we simply want to hike and scale the largest mountain rock face in Oceania. It just didn't make sense.

After what seemed hours, one of Denny's employees came inside and showed the immigration official that we had permits to climb Carstensz. After much screaming back and forth, an Immigration officer took pictures of our passports and returned them to us.

I had to remind myself that we were in a foreign country that just a few years ago didn't think twice about shooting foreigners, and that a few decades before that, went to arms against Australia to fight for independence. I guess we were being seen as an enemy; with the military presence and army tank at the airport a clear sign of intimidation.

The Chinese group also had their passports confiscated and eventually given back as well.

After we left the airport we were ushered into two separate vehicles with Denny's team and driven to the hotel. Here we would rest until yet another early morning flight to where we would start our trek.

Our hotel was newly built. Its modern structure was a stark contrast to the favela neighbourhood in which it was located in.

That afternoon we had to go to the Immigration Office to fill out paperwork for our permits to climb Carstensz. I didn't understand this step since we had already provided our pictures and shown our permits at the airport. Regardless, we went to the Immigration Office, had our pictures taken and paperwork signed. Again. I guess when in Rome...

Here I took the opportunity to enquire again if any other Portuguese woman or man had climbed Carstensz. I was assured that records are now kept and they did not have anyone from that country recorded in that office. The only other office where permits could be obtained would be Naribe, however the officer seemed to believe no other Portuguese person had climbed, and certain no other Portuguese woman had.

They were right, no other Portuguese woman had done it, I was the first, however Angelo Felgueiras successfully summited Carstensz before me, so technically I became the second person Portuguese person.

After our visit to immigration, we went shopping for a few necessities; umbrellas and food for what was supposed to be for me, the only vegetarian in the group. Cans of beans and some corn was the only supplement to what I thought would surely be a nutritious diet provided by the touring company. I now appreciate my sarcasm as I edit this page and sip on a vintage 2015 bottle of Portuguese white wine and munch on chips and pico de gallo.

Denny then informs us that our toilet and shower tent, which we had been assured to have, had been stolen from base camp, so we would not have one. Are you kidding me? Climbing with no privacy to shower or use the bathroom!?

As a businessperson, I didn't understand this. If this tent was stolen during another group's expedition, then I would expect they would just go buy another one. At this point though we decided to take an "Oh well" attitude and move on.

Then at last, we had a group dinner and rested for the night before going to the airport to catch the small plane that would take us to Sugapa.

October 4 was Steve's birthday. I was sad and conflicted that I missed it and it tugged at my heart. I missed Patricia and Nicole, Ethan and Julia, and Daisy, but the anticipation of the climb was pumping through my veins and keeping me focused. I had the familiarity of Emmanuel, so I didn't feel completely alone... I would encounter that later on other mountains.

When we arrived at the landing strip in Sugapa, all the YouTube videos I had previously seen came to life. There were hordes of motorcycle riders, ready and eager to get your business. After lots of negotiation from our local guides, we each got on the back of a motorcycle including duffle bags, all our supplies, and tents. Quite the sight! I was waiting for a film crew to shout out "cut" at any moment.

We made several stops along the way. The first two were close together and were to pay off local government authorities and the local government army office. It was straight out of a movie scene, especially when you add the army office in the local village, with a wooden house and a handful of spectators, one of which was a naked native wearing only a koteka (also referred to as a horim or penis gourd). The koteka is a penis sheath traditionally worn by native male inhabitants of some (mainly highland) ethnic groups in New Guinea, Indonesia to cover their penises.

At another roadblock, maybe our third but honestly I lost count, we were blocked by local tribe members. It was very intense, to the point it actually seemed staged. Staged and choreographed to scare and rip off foreigners that is! Even the local army guy, who we had been paid off less than half an hour before at stop number two, had to be brought in and threats were made. Eventually we were let through and were able to continue our trip. ALOT of money greased their palms during this long process and we also lost our kitchen tent at this roadblock, we later learned.

Finally, we arrived at the leader of the Dani tribes' farm, where we spent the night. This was also from whom we hired our porters the next day.

We stayed in two local wood homes, which had three rooms. We slept in our sleeping bags on the floor, while it rained all night. We spent time with the local children staring at our food and us. Was I having fun yet?

William was the local leader. His farmhouses accommodated guests such as us. He had 7 wives and countless children. Yes, I said 7. William claims to be a Christian but ahh, no, I don't think so.

Was this what I had signed up for? Did I sign up for all of this tiring travel, negotiating, being treated with suspicion and having meagre living arrangements, all before we have even started to climb? It was. And this was only the beginning.

The day after we arrived at Williams' farm, we got up at 7:00 am local time but only started hiking around 11:00 am. It took several hours for the bidding and organization of the porter team. I was told we had 19 porters but it was hard to say. Each porter traveled with their whole family; the husband, wife and children.

The head of the Dani tribe, William stood in the middle of his farm, and after having an argument in public with one of his seven wives, he started selecting porters. Once selected, each was given a blue pouch, which I assumed had some information about what they were carrying and whom it belonged to, and a bag to carry. The porters each carried one of our duffle bags, our supplies and our tents.

William also put out a "work order" to the villagers that attended this work assignment meeting, for those selected members of the tribe to go ahead of us and repair some sections of the trail that had been affected by a recent mudslide. This I was told by Raymond, our local head guide, was to cost us the equivalent of $400.00 US dollars.

I had a two person tent to myself, which I had chosen specifically to have more room so that I wouldn't feel so claustrophobic. It was a luxury to be alone; it gave me the opportunity to journal, to write some of the notes that supported this book. It was also a perfect introduction to my life as a mountaineer!

Raymond led a prayer before we left. This would be a daily ritual, which I appreciated. Back home, Raymond is a non-practicing Pastor and his wife is the lead Pastor of their local church. The trail was demanding, as we had to navigate up and down wet, rocky terrain, tree stumps and even rushing rivers. At one point, as we were walking along the riverbank after a previous scary crossing, I could hear the raging waters and I started to feel anxious. But then up ahead I saw a bridge. What a beautiful sight! I was so happy and relieved, I got giddy!

The trail demands your complete attention, one distraction and you fall. I tripped once, the first day. Many more would follow....

One day, our fellow climber Philipe decided he had had enough, and would be returning the next morning with one of the guides, Hata. He opted to fly again to Timika and would take the helicopter option to base camp. The steep cost of this choice was $6,000.00 USD! His plan was to meet us at base camp and then attempt to Summit with us. He planned to return to Timika via helicopter as well. I secretly envied him. It was daunting and exhausting. But I was also pleased to experience the trek. I had trained hard and was up for the challenge!

I had to keep reminding myself that I was doing this, both to accomplish something very challenging and also, to be the first Portuguese woman to climb Carstensz Pyramid. This climb was primarily for my mom and to raise money for mental health. These goals kept me going. And in retrospect, I know I learned so much about mountaineering on this trip. And about myself.

Several times, during my hike and when certain sections were scary, I knew Jesus had me in his care. I felt secure. In a way, climbing was my path to Jesus.

At the end of the day, reaching camp and being able to contact my family was an incentive and a huge comfort. I missed them. I truly did. I was the only woman on the expedition and even though my tent was always erected first and all the guys were great, attentive, helpful and true gentlemen, I still felt at the end of the day that I could have used a hug, and some company in the tent. Emmanuel had told me he didn't like being alone in a tent when he climbed because one needs to ward off loneliness. I had shrugged it off then, but when I finished climbing the 7 Summits, I agreed one hundred per cent with him. In Carstensz, he and Adam shared a tent. The rest of us had our own.

The next day promised to be an especially hard one. Juan, another one of our local guides who was leading us, kept saying, "Hard, lots of mud!" He was not kidding.

One never expects to eat gourmet meals while trekking. However, there are several options of freeze dry foods, such as those by Mountain House. And there are other lighter weight food options that make long expedition nutrition reasonable.

I am still not certain why, if it was the remoteness of Carstensz Pyramid, the harsh condition of trekking in, or the necessity of using local porters all the way, but nutrition was a HUGE issue, especially for me as a vegetarian.

Here, the first day when we set out from the Dani tribe camp, we were handed a box of chocolate cookies and a smaller box of another variety of cookies. I thought it was a joke. But no! It was our lunch. The remaining lunches throughout the expedition varied the type of cookie box and then we graduated to a chocolate bar to accompany it. Every mountain I learned has its challenges, nutrition during this expedition was a big issue.

For breakfast we had a slice of white bread and a one egg omelet. There was a jar of Nutella on the table from one of our expedition members and I offer a jar of dehydrated peanut butter I also had brought, in spite of weight limitations. That was it. Nothing else.

We also warmed ourselves with ready mixes of flavored cappuccinos! Loaded up on sugar!

Rice and ramen noodles were our daily staple for dinner. To this day I have a hard time with rice dishes and I can't stand noodles, especially ramen noodles. The guys had fried spam with some dinners and canned fish. At base camp, they had chicken wings and one night, prawns. I saw an ice box there and it was below 0 in temperature, plus the supplies came via helicopter, so I knew it was possible to have proper food!

I had some of the corn and beans we bought in Timika, or at least I did the times the beans were not mixed in with meat! I still remember Emmanuel telling Raymond and Juan the purpose of me being a vegetarian was I did not eat meat, so cooking the beans with the meat was not the right thing to do.

At base camp I did have steamed green vegetables added to my rice and noodles on a couple of occasions. A massive treat!

I was thankful I had packed some granola bars, despite being advised against it because of the extra weight. I put some in my backpack since a porter carried the duffle bag to the next camp. I'm so glad I did! Adam share one or two of his with me too.

On what was our second day of trekking, we learned our routine for the next several days. We got up for breakfast at 7 am but only hit the "road" at 9 am or so. There were always negotiations with the porters regarding load allocations, and as a result we had to remove some stuff from all our bags each day to keep up with the changing daily rules.

The whole trail was hard. There were so many tree roots that it was similar to rock climbing, but on trees. At one point I got my red UGG rain boot stuck in the mud and my foot came right out. I remembered seeing this in a YouTube video, and despite the warning, here I was…stuck in the mud. We reached camp late that day. It was about 6:35 pm and I was finally in my tent. It was raining, as was the pattern every evening. I was cold and tired and just want to cuddle in my sleeping bag.

Every day I toyed with the idea of telling Emmanuel I wanted to take the helicopter return option after we summited. I couldn't imagine retracing my steps on the return and having to walk on the treacherous terrain.

My stomach hurt a little. I was starting to feel the effects of all the sugar I was consuming. Our bodies just aren't built to survive on cookies and chocolate bars. Duh!

Every evening Raymond and Juan would say that day was the hardest part of climbing Carstensz. But then they would warn us that tomorrow would involve lots of mud.

"Really? More than today?" I kept silently asking myself.

Many times, I shed tears, but mercifully no one saw. This happened on every mountain. If any of the guides saw, no one every commented. I am sure everyone was fighting their own feelings, fatigue and thoughts.

One of the days midway, we got hit with a storm and climbing in the rain was really hard. My rain boots got completed soaked and I knew I would start my next day with wet feet. It was brutal.

Not only were we "rock climbing" on tree roots, but with the added rain it became a really hard trek. I kept thinking about Steve telling me about the people he read about online "crawling to climb". Well, I can tell you it was an accurate account. There was no graceful way of climbing over all those roots!

I had to remind myself several times that Jesus had me in the palm of his hand and that I would display the flag I had made for my trip to Mount Rainier. I knew I would take his flag to the summit and have a picture with it saying "Jesus Rocks!"

With those thoughts came the peace and willpower to continue towards the base of Carstensz Pyramid, and eventually to climb it. With perseverance came the opportunity to also marvel at the beautiful landscape that surrounded us. Along with the rainforest and muddy trails, I had the opportunity to see gold dust flowing from the Freeport mine. The landscape with basically non-existing wildlife, other than the occasional bird, was impressive. I felt privileged and certainly blessed to have seen it and have trekked through it. Today mountaineers wanting to climb Carstensz can no longer hike in. They can only helicopter in and out. We were one of the last groups to do so, as things stand.

It was exhausting, and yet, on some level, exhilarating. My excitement was fueled by what was to come.

After 5 days, I was tired of stepping in mud. I was tired of the trekking. I just wanted to go to base camp.

In fact, I was uncomfortably hungry and my body was showing signs of rejecting the rice, noodles and cookies, which were the only things I was feeding it. Unknown to me at the time, I was starting to experience signs of altitude sickness, as my hands and face began to swell up. I didn't have a mirror on this expedition, though I learned to take one onwards, but looking back at photos, I know it was around this time I had started to experience symptoms. I ended up looking like a chipmunk!

The countless sugary cappuccino mixes I drench my body with also threatened to be expelled. Uh oh!

At the end of day five, we camped at Nasidome. The view was incredible. We could see Puncak Jaya and Carstensz just behind it. It's a wow moment! The morning sunrise greeted us teasingly, to entice us to continue over the New Zealand pass that awaited us, and then we would finally arrive at base camp. We were now at 3,734 metres (about 12,250 feet above sea level).

Only a few porters would proceed with us to take our supplies to base camp. The rest would remain here and wait. Three of our young porters posed for a picture with the perfect backdrop!

This was our first introduction to a lot of rock! The New Zealand pass stands at approximately 4,500 metres (approximately 14,700 feet above sea level) and represented our next big challenge. We had to scramble up a rock face, free style. THAT is not easy folks! We were getting tired as we had trekked on rocks and rocky pathways up and down, up and down for hours. Argh!

We also had to be careful with loose rock, both as a courtesy and potential danger for those behind us. The pace was slower than I'd like, but necessary. It truly was a team effort keeping tabs on what's up ahead and what's going on behind you.

We arrived at what was supposed to be base camp. Aside from the aquamarine small lake, which was stunning, it didn't look much like the vision on YouTube. The rest of base camp was filled with garbage. God's beautiful creation was a bit of a muck heap! And it was cold.

The seventh day in the mountain was our much planned for and awaited day. At last, we would attempt to climb Carstensz Pyramid. Yay!

We learned however there was another camp set at the base of Carstensz called Yellow Valley, and involved another 90 minutes of hiking, on rocky ground of course! We needed to do this trek before summiting.

As we settled in for the night I finally told Emmanuel I wanted to take the helicopter back after our summit with Philippe; that I did not want to trek out. No way was I going through that mud and those tree roots again! After my announcement, JP said he wanted to as well. We all ended up taking the Heli down. I think all the guys were just waiting for the "girl" to cave so they didn't have to express what they wanted to do. I really didn't care.

We got up at about midnight and started trekking, wearing our summit day clothes. We headed towards the other base camp, next to the first rope for Carstensz.

Unfortunately, it was raining. And it was steady.

Once we arrived, Raymond guided us into a large common tent to wait out the rain. We were met by Philippe, who had arrived via helicopter the previous day along with Hata, the third local guide. Raymond says we would wait until about 6 or 7 am to see if the rain stops.

It does not.

All the other guys and guides call Emmanuel "Manu". I didn't and don't. He doesn't actually like it. To me, he was "Emm" which is for short Emmanuel, or I simply used his full name. Emm who was our Terra Ultima guide and Raymond our Lead local guide, made the decision to return to our base camp and try again the next day, as they said it was too dangerous to climb in the rain. I was very disappointed by this news. We trekked back. I won't share my inner dialogue at the time, though I will share that in Everest four and a half years later because sometimes it could not be held in.

It rained all day. I spent the whole day alone in my tent. I was able to watch "The Choice" that I had downloaded to my iPad, at least until the battery died, to help pass the time. Because of the lack of sun, my solar charger didn't work very well and all my charges were conserved for my iPhone and inReach devices so I could communicate with my family. They were my lifeline and what kept me feeling some connection to reality through this whole adventure.

It was as we walked back from a non-summit day that Emmanuel decided that he too would take the helicopter back along with Adam. Myself, JP and Philippe already planned to do it so it was a relief to know that once we summited, we wouldn't be facing that long muddy trek back to civilization. Emmanuel called Terra Ultima on the sat phone and informed them, so that arrangements could be made with Denny.

I think the rain, dampness, coldness and lack of food choices and proper nutrition was taking a toll on all of us. I know it was for me.

Raymond then proceeded to advise William's brother who had stay with us as a point of contact between us and the porters, of our intention, and arrangements were made to have the porters dismissed.

We had provided Emmanuel with our share of the tips and he gave them to the porters. All this happened while I was inside my tent, as the rain never stopped.

At dinner time we realized the porters had taken JP's boots and Adam's umbrella. It was raining; we needed that umbrella! Emmanuel was annoyed. Raymond said nothing could be done, as the porters had already left.

I remember that I was feeling exhausted and didn't care much. I wanted to go climb the rock face, summit and go home as quickly as possible! I was so close to accomplishing my goal, but I still needed to finish what I came to do.

My internal voice was saying, "Come on Ema, you are almost there. Let's do this!"

When the night was clear, we took off again from our base camp and trekked to the first rope. My stomach was nervous and my body was fighting back. Much like an angry child, my body chose the worst time possible to throw a tantrum. I had to make two stops during the trek to urgently relieve myself. Some things you would rather not do while tied into the rope with a gentleman, at close quarters, on Carstensz's rock face but I will skip the details.

Later Emm would make reference to this event, saying "what happens in Carstensz stays in Carstensz", when trying to assess my health on my first attempt on Everest.

The climb was hard, but more than hard, it was long. We climbed up aided by our jumars clipped into fixed ropes that had been put in place. There were two sets of ropes on some sections; one of the rope's integrity was questionable so a second was added. Each member of our group had a dedicated guide. One member, Adam, is an expert and strong rock climber; he has climbed several rock faces with a 5.12 grade difficulty. He was assigned to Raymond, our head local guide. Raymond had climbed Carstensz more than forty times. They were the fastest duo and were in front. Philippe was climbing with Hata, and they had started before us, since they were already at the closer base camp, at the base of the mountain. However, once Adam and Raymond caught up to them, they went ahead and took the lead as planned. JP had been partnered with Juan and then Emmanuel took on the challenge of guiding me up.

I was and will always be eternally grateful for his patience and for him diligently helping me as needed. A couple of times he even offered his leg as a prop for me to climb over a rock face; being short has its pitfalls! We were a team that day – tied to the same rope. Our safety and success required we worked as a team. I listened to him closely. I knew he was not doing this selfishly for himself to summit Carstensz. He was there to ensure I had the best chance of succeeding myself, as his client, and as his friend. He encouraged me several times during our climb, stating how great I was doing and that we were making excellent time. I didn't quite believe him, but I needed to hear that and appreciated his kind words. I was in this with him and I trusted him. I was at a point in my life where I needed to learn to start trusting again. Trusting others and trusting myself. This was teaching me that.

I have since had the opportunity at home to listen to video comments he made along the way. His praises for me are heartwarming. He was ready to forgo his chance of a lifetime to summit if I was not able.

I later learned on that day, as he was telling Adam about our climb, that he had doubts that we would summit because of my fear of heights. I appreciated that Emmanuel had such a great poker face on the mountain!

During our ascent using the jumar, he had me reciting – "jumar, step up, jumar, step up, jumar, step up". Oh, and he reminded me several times to breath! A lesson I took with me to a few other mountains.

When we approached the Tyrolean Traverse, I was literally terrified. Walking on a steel cable suspended thousands of feet in the air and only held by two security lines from my harness, each attached to a carabiner, I started to have a panic attack. I had promised to "communicate" during this climb, especially after breaking three ribs during training at Mount Tremblant and climbing all day back in May without saying a word. So, I told Emmanuel I was having a panic attack and I could feel my throat tighten. He quickly helped me by responding with a calming tone of voice. We stopped for a moment. He calmly instructed me to slow down my breathing. Once I accomplished that, he gently explained how to walk on the rope and where to focus my attention and emphasized the magic words that I would not fall. And if I did, I would only hang on the rope and he would be able to come get me. I am certain now it would not be possible had it happened but then I believed him. It sure helps having a Toronto Paramedic for a guide and as my best friend!

He assured me I was secure on the ropes and then firmly told me I could do it! I wanted and needed to cross this and summit. With my heart stuck in my throat, I followed his instructions and started self-talking to myself saying "duck feet, duck feet" as I moved one foot at a time on the steel cable. Suddenly I had completed the whole traverse! As happy as I was, and even though I heard Emmanuel's praises on the other end, I realized I would have to repeat it on the way back. Somehow, I cleared my mind enough to focus on the rocks and narrow path ahead.

We did stop at some point, I can't quite remember exactly where, and looked around us. The view was incredible! At 16,000 feet up in the air, the sunrise was amazing and the clean crispness of the various rock faces was breathtaking. It's amazing what God creates for us. Even through my anxiety, I could see and finally understand why mountaineers climb! It was surreal in its beauty.

Walking, secured on the rope, but without the jumar was easier and faster, and we were able to do this in some sections. There were two literal "leaps of faith" that we were required to jump before reaching the summit; meaning you need to jump from one rock point to another with open air below. Yes, you hook a carabiner from your lanyard attached to your harness as a security onto a few fixed ropes, but let's be honest, the rock was hard and sharp. If you miss the jump, you may not fall to the bottom, but it was going to hurt hitting your body against either rock! I could imagine my face getting cut – and it's not like I am not accident-prone! I am the one that broke 3 ribs on a bathtub just before a training day in Canada a few months ago! AND I have short legs and jumps are a greater challenge for me! I really, really didn't think I could do it.

Again, my anxiety was so high, all I can remember is Emmanuel telling me to breathe.

"Calm down Ema!".

He went first. He explained to me what I needed to do, how I had my back-up line, and then he added that he would be there to catch me if I needed it. Even though he was working as our guide, this was his first time in Carstensz as well. I did not want to be responsible for him not reaching the summit because he had to take care of me. This thought motivated me. So, I followed his instructions that he was repeating from the other side. Just when my hand was falling short of reaching the last handhold on the rock, he grabbed my hand, and pulled me up. Phew – he caught me! Ditto for the second gap. Talk about feeling like your life was in someone else's hands! Emm had told me he had me, and he did.

Suddenly music came to our ears...our colleagues' ecstatic screams of happiness at reaching the top of Carstensz Pyramid! We cheered with them! They were at the summit point. The sky was blue, but clouds were moving fast towards the mountain. This was a daily occurrence and predictable weather pattern; it's why we started so early. The summit point still seemed far for us. But a few minutes later, as Adam and Raymond started to descend, Adam assured us we were only minutes away! Climbing and descending Carstensz is rope dependent, and only one person can pass on a rope at each point. We had eight in our group, therefore Raymond did not want to waste time hanging around the Summit point.

We continued excitedly and as we see Filipe waiting for the others, just a few feet down from the summit point, we pushed up and reached the Summit ourselves. I cried. Emmanuel was first shocked and then ecstatic. He laughed as he wipe my tears off my face. Hata and Juan were still on the summit point and helped us take many pictures. Juan captured our arrival to the summit point on video, which he sent to me. I am so glad he did because in all honesty, it was all quite a blur. All I remember is being there. And being elated. But the video proved it was real; I had climbed my first mountain.

I fumbled with my inReach GPS device. I had it programmed with an automatic message that would tell everyone we were on top of Carstensz. I couldn't find it. AGHHHHHH! Emmanuel told me to breathe, relax and take five minutes and look. We had time. But I was shaking. I was only able to share our location and hoped anyone following us could see we were on top of Carstensz Pyramid, the highest point in Oceania. We were at the summit. We were actually at the summit. Then it was time to come down. Same route, same way. JP guided by Juan, and Philippe guided by Hata were in front of us.

Again, I listened to Emmanuel's instructions on the two leaps of faith, because when I saw JP having difficulty with one of them, I panicked. Emmanuel said I had it! And with his help, I did.

We had about 600 feet of rappels to do. We were using our ACT's, as we normally did in Canada, even though our Indonesian guides used a figure 8 device, even though it may not be so foolproof for the type of ropes on Carstensz, it was supposedly easier. The ropes however got so wet and therefore harden, so I don't know if it mattered but trust me, the descent was hard.

Then it started to snow. Yup! Snow. After the snow, because we were descending in altitude, it began to rain. I started thinking about hypothermia as just a few days prior to us reaching base camp a climber had died. The blue tarp was still in the side of the mountain, where his body had been found.

"Try to think positively Ema. It's okay. You'll be okay." I told myself as I tried to manage my thoughts.

The rope was hard to insert into our ACT's. Emmanuel helped me with many of mine. He would secure himself at each transfer point, get the rope on his ACT, then I would secure my line, on the transfer point, and we would secure the same rope on my ACT device. This allowed us to be faster; as soon as he was done with that rope, I would be ready to go. He always double checked our set-up. Safety was a priority.

I was getting cold and wet. We had JP and Philippe in front of us, so at each new rope section I would start to get cold as we stood still, waiting for the line to be free. I felt my body was getting unreasonably chilly and when I checked why, I realized my Gortex pants were not secured properly. The only thing holding them from falling down my waist was my harness. I had not secured them properly when I had needed a bathroom break earlier on the mountain and I had not realized it. I tried to secure them properly, however, it was too late – I was already wet. Ugh.

After a few rappels, I started to feel short of breath. Each time I leaned back on my harness while on the line, I felt like the air was being sucked out of me. My left side hurt. It was like someone had punched me. After trying to adjust myself on each new rappel to see if the pain would ease and breathing would be better, I finally told Emmanuel, and he immediately requested my backpack. I did not think that was the problem, but I gave it to him and he put it inside his.

Removing my backpack changed nothing. My left side continued to constrict my breathing with each rappel. But I knew I needed to move and to move fast when the rope was free. Waiting for the rope allowed me to breathe, even though I just wanted to move and get down. I suppressed my urge to ask Emmanuel for us to go ahead of Philippe. He was our group guide and was instructing and encouraging Philippe at the same time. We were a team after all, and the team works together and was there for each other. Emmanuel's leadership impressed me. I realized Francois-Xavier had sent Terra Ultima's best guide, for their first expedition to Carstensz Pyramid.

Finally, we were on the very last rope. Emmanuel secured himself, then called out to me to come secure myself on the line next to his as we would repel side by side and get off the mountain at the same time. I was a little puzzled, but he said – "Let's have some fun!"

Once I was ready on the second line, which we had determined was solid, we started rappelling in parallel on the rock. Wet and tired after being on the mountain for more than 12 hours, my friend Emmanuel said with a huge smile "Ready?" and I signaled yes.

"On the count of 3", he added, "1, 2, 3". We did a last jump and landed off the mountain at the same time.

It was my first summit. And for it, I am forever indebted to my best friend Emmanuel.

CHAPTER 6
ALTITUDE SICKNESS

When I got back home and looked at the Carstensz Pyramid summit pictures, my face was puffy. I didn't look like myself. I actually looked like a chipmunk.

We had summited without a lunch break, only sipping on water. We ascended and descended the mountain for 12 hours straight.

I know I became dehydrated. We had been expecting a celebratory meal when we reached the tents at Yellow Valley (the base camp close to the first rope on Carstensz), but when we arrived, we only rested briefly and made our way to our base camp. It was another 90-minute trek to my tent. I was exhausted but happy to be able to change into dry clothes. It was my last pair of everything. My teammates were looking concerned as they gazed at my swollen face and squinting eyes. Something was wrong.

The plan however was to leave the next morning and go to Timika, as the helicopter was picking us up. It was not what happened.

The morning after our summit of Carstensz Pyramid, Raymond received a report that the weather in Timika was bad and there would be no helicopter that day.

I had woken with my face noticeably swollen and the left side of my back, in my kidney area, was painful to the slightest touch. I was desperate to leave the mountain.

I accepted that we would hopefully be leaving the next day. I told myself I could manage for another day. I texted Steve to let him know, as well as my family. When he responded, he said he had read that a group took 6 days to get off the mountain and I silently started to panic. I was worried about my health and starting to feel trapped. Thoughts raced in my head. What if I had to wait for a week? What if I started to get very ill?

I felt powerless. I didn't know what to do because ultimately, there was nothing I could do but wait.

As a group, we decided to move from our base camp to the other Yellow Valley base camp, so we would be with Philippe, our other teammate and also so we would be on site when the helicopter came. It would also be less challenging for the pilot having only one stop to make. The pilot was new, as the 3-month switch over had just occurred. Raymond wanted to spare us his worries, but we later found out first-hand how inexperienced the new pilot was.

The following day, the weather in Timika was reportedly good, however, we had to wait 3 hours for the clouds to clear in Carstensz. They did not. All helicopter rides were cancelled at 9:30 am and I was crushed. We had summited two days ago and we were still waiting to leave. I turned on my inReach GPS and sent a quick text to Steve and my family that read: "Weather bad. No helicopter. I am OK. Turning GPS off. Little battery. Love you." I then turned the inReach off because we couldn't recharge our devices since we hadn't had enough sun to charge them. I felt stranded.

Emmanuel had started monitoring my water intake the day before and had me on antibiotics, but my hands were very swollen, my face was swollen, and my left kidney was screaming in pain. He borrowed the satellite phone from our local guides and had called Sunnybrook Hospital in Toronto to ask for additional advice on how to treat me. Did I mention he is a Toronto Paramedic? Not everyone gets to climb with a paramedic. I had two - Emmanuel and my other teammate, Adam.

I felt like a nuisance. I was alone and sick. I tried not to cry but I did. I was the only female in the entire camp and I was crying, and crying made me feel even worse. My teammates however didn't judge me. They were actually all very attentive and even taught me how to play poker and "presidents". We played many card games to pass the time since we were essentially trapped. We also listened to music and were surprised that Philippe had an amazing music collection on his phone!

As I lay in the general tent the second day, inside my sleeping bag, the guys relaxed taking turns playing various card games. Suddenly, we heard a commotion outside. I thought we were being rescued, but it was only fifteen volunteers from Freeport Mine that had arrived to clean up the garbage at base camp. When they finished, the mine helicopter would do a flyby and pick up the garbage bags they had secured together. Heavy sigh.

Emmanuel went outside to talk to them. Unknown to me at that point, it seemed that morning I looked really bad, perhaps as bad as I felt, and my teammates were very worried. I should have figured it out when Emmanuel had called Toronto from the base camp, but then I just thought he was being super sweet and conscientious. He didn't want a client to die!

He had also moved me from my private tent into the main group tent, where he, Adam and JP had slept the previous night. Emmanuel had said it was easier to keep an eye on me there. JP took my tent and I took JP's spot. I was grateful to be monitored.

My sleeping bag was sandwiched between the sleeping bags of Emmanuel and Adam. I would not get this well treated on any other mountain, but then I wasn't sick like this either...until Everest that is.

Emmanuel had gone out to talk to the leader of the volunteer group and explained he had a Canadian client who was very ill. Together they determined that if our helicopter did not come the next day, I would need to activate my SOS button on my inReach GPS device. The SOS would be picked up in Jakarta and forwarded to Freeport Mine. Freeport Mine emergency personnel would then come and take me to the mines' medical facility to be accessed by their medical team. From there I would be transferred to Timika, depending on my situation, either by air or car.

It helped immensely to do some name dropping with the volunteer leader, as this was communicated to the pit mine leader. I was thankful for my Canadian passport and for Emmanuel's ex-girlfriend, who was the mine's current chief geologist. I was thankful my best friend had this connection.

At the time, Freeport Mine operated the Grasberg Mine in Papua, near Puncak Jaya, Carstensz Pyramid. Freeport Mine employed 30,000 local Indonesians and was the largest gold mine and the second largest copper mine in the world, though they have since pulled their operations from the area.

When Juan brought us our dinner at the end of the day, it was notably very little. Juan apologized, but we told him not to worry and asked if he was ok. He sounded and seemed sick but he just smiled and assured us that he was fine.

The small amount of food didn't bother us; no one felt like eating anyway. We just wanted to get off the mountain. What we didn't know, fortunately at the time, was that we had run out of food.

That evening, Raymond came into our common tent and said that Denny had messaged him to say the next day's weather forecast looked good in Timika, and that hopefully the mountain would be clear as well. The flight time down the mountain only takes 30 minutes.

Denny had given instructions that the first 3 off the mountain would be me, JP and Philippe. The second team to come off the mountain would be Adam, Emmanuel and Hata. Then followed by Raymond and Juan on another flight.

As Raymond spoke those words, I saw Adams' heart drop. He was as desperate as I was to get out of base camp. The only difference between us was that I was puffed up like a balloon and had signs of severe edema in my lower legs and feet, hands and face.

Emmanuel hesitated and then told Raymond that he might need to change the plan, depending on my condition, as he or Adam would need to go with me to a private hospital. He was adamant that he would not leave any client behind, so it would have to be Adam, which was the original plan.

Then it was Philippe's turn to worry. Adam jokingly commented to Emmanuel, how easy it was to get him off the flight. Emmanuel answered firmly, "Well, I can't show favoritism".

I realized then how hard the past few days had been for him. He was Adam's good friend and a fellow paramedic but at that moment, he was also his guide. He was my friend and fellow member of the board at Peaks for Change Foundation, but here he was my guide and I was his sick client.

Emmanuel asked for Raymond's reassurance regarding the next day's weather. As Raymond got up from his seat, and exited the tent, he said, "Well Eman, you better pray to God the weather is good tomorrow and pray hard!"

I woke up in the middle of the night to use the washroom. Outside, the sky above was clear and the stars bright. I knew this meant nothing, as in the morning clouds could move in quickly. I had been begging Jesus to provide help; to bring the helicopter. And not just begging - crying, pleading, praying, over and over. I wanted to be home with my family more deeply than I could ever remember. Please, Lord.

As I lay down again, Emmanuel stirred from his sleeping bag and asked me how the weather looked outside. I told him it was clear and he replied, "Good, I had been wanting to check, but I was just too afraid."

As morning approached, I couldn't stop myself from pleading more and begging Jesus in my head. "Please, please, please," I repeated like a mantra.

Soon it was official; the helicopter would take off from Timika with 3 passengers from Alpine Accents that had been waiting to come up to base camp to climb. Myself, JP and Philippe would be going back down.

When Raymond said the helicopter would arrive in 20 minutes, we packed up in 5. The sense of relief was overwhelming. At last, I was going home.

The helicopter arrived at about 6:30 am. We were ready to go; more than ready! As the helicopter landed, three guys, who dressed and looked like they all belonged in a GQ magazine, came out and immediately turned their gaze up to Carstensz. As soon as I got over the fact that they looked like models, it occurred to me that they were in shorts and t-shirts, and it was at least minus 10 at base camp!

They were in for a rude awakening! I was wearing three layers of clothing and my Gortex jacket over that. I had slept with long johns and two layers of clothing and two hot water bottles. I shook my head. I noticed an expensive camera around one of the guy's necks and his gaze transfixed on the beautiful Carstensz Pyramid. It suddenly occurred to me; yes, it was indeed a beautiful mountain. But now I was desperate to get away from it as quickly as possible.

I was delighted and relieved to finally be sitting in the helicopter. I could see that our pilot was very nervous and noted the co-pilot was giving him instructions on speed and how to turn around. I assumed the co-pilot was an instructor. Then I recalled that Philippe had commented that the pilot that brought him and Hata up, was nervous and constantly asking for oxygen. We had the same pilot. Philippe was right. This new pilot was visibly anxious, but for some reason, I didn't care. I was going home.

The view during the ride was amazing. We got to see the mountains and the Freeport Mine. The sky was blue and we were surrounded by soft white clouds.

The Chinese guys, back at the airport 11 days ago, had been right. Why trek when you can fly?! But I must say, the waiting game for the helicopter and dependence on the ever-changing weather can be more maddening and demoralizing then trekking in deep mud. At least trekking you are doing something, moving and feel somewhat in control!

Sitting in base camp, cold, hungry, and very ill, after a successful summit can crush you. It crushed me ... and my spirit. I felt a vacuum empty of hope.

Once on the ground, we learned our pilot couldn't drive much better. For unknown reasons when we landed in Timika, he decided to chauffeur us to the terminal, and made our car driver walk across the tarmac. It seemed clear, the pilot was wasting time. So much so that he was only able to do one more flight to drop off 3 more climbers, and pick up Emmanuel, Adam, and Hata. By the time they returned to Timika, the weather in Carstensz had turned and no more flights were attempted.

Climbers waiting to go up remained in Timika and those waiting to come down, remained in Carstensz, stranded. I worried about Juan and Raymond. Meanwhile, Denny booked a flight for the five of us the same afternoon (1:00 pm) to return to Denpasar, Bali.

We arrived in Bali on October 15, 2017 around 6:00 pm and checked again into the Ramada, our groups' hotel, and had a celebratory dinner. It all felt surreal.

I left Bali on October 16, 2017, on KLM, at 8:40 pm local time, headed for home, anxious to see my family and be in my own bed.

As I sat on the plane headed for home, my feet were pounding. I felt the pressure in my legs. I could actually feel the swelling. My hands were no longer swollen or my face, but my legs were. I would need to figure this out and see if this was due to altitude because Kilimanjaro would be higher.

I had not taken Diamox in Carstensz, a tablet used to prevent or reduce altitude sickness symptoms. I did end up taking it for all the other peaks, except Kosciusko and then Everest - the Summit. Looking back to Carstensz I am convinced, I was suffering with a form of altitude sickness.

CHAPTER 7
KILIMANJARO

When I returned from Carstensz, my family Doctor ran several test and even called a high altitude specialist in the United States. Against medical advice, I decided to go ahead with plans to climb Kilimanjaro.

Kilimanjaro is the highest mountain in Africa, reaching 5,895 metres (19,341 ft) above sea level. The first persons known to have reached the summit of the mountain were Hans Meyer and Ludwig Purtscheller in 1889. The mountain, part of Kilimanjaro National Park, is a major tourist destination. It is estimated that 25,000 people visit Kilimanjaro yearly to try to climb it. It is also estimated that only 66% actually reach the summit.

I think the reason so many people attempt it, is because it is one of the least technical peaks. Kilimanjaro is a hike; mind you a long hike, and the majority of people that climb Kilimanjaro have no aspirations to climb any other mountains. This leads to minimal training to prepare for the climb by many, and them being ill prepared for even the weather not to mention potential altitude sickness. Climbing "Kili" as it is often called, is a tourist attraction.

For years Steve had wanted climb Kilimanjaro. Every year as we planned a vacation, it came up as a possible destination. Let's climb Kilimanjaro and then go and do a Safari. It's what everyone does he would say.

To be honest I dismissed it many times. Climbing mountains had not been my thing as you know now.

But here I was, a mountaineer in the making. I knew I wanted to climb Kilimanjaro. I also knew that successfully summiting Kilimanjaro required training, and a visit to the travel clinic as well.

I agreed to climb Kilimanjaro with Steve, but with each training hike we attempted I got frustrated. From Steve's dismissal of the health precautions needed to successfully climb to his selfishness during training hikes, I felt my anxiety level raise each day.

Our first training hike together was in Collingwood, Blue Mountain, Ontario during the August 2017 civic holiday, long weekend. I had figured it was a good time to go for a hike together, as I was also still training for Carstensz. As we started, he would walk really fast, and then stop, hyperventilating, out of breath. I tried telling him to walk slower, to practice his pace and to hike with me along-side, as a teammate. Well, we ended up in a huge fight and when we were descending the ski hill, he literally almost ran down it, leaving me to hike alone. His excuse was that it was too hot, he was sweating a lot and he wanted to get out of the sun. I cried most of the way down, alone.

Our second training hike was about a month before we were scheduled to go to Tanzania. I had asked him to come out for a hike at Rattlesnake Conservation area so he would have a chance to break in his hiking boots. While I was getting ready the morning we had planned to go, he announced he wanted to go to the gym first. I got upset, and then decided I would let it go and would wait an hour for him to finish. Two hours later he finally came home and puttered around asking what he needed. I was furious. It was two hours past the time I would usually go out and train. I felt disrespected and couldn't believe how selfish he was being.

This was the first of many instances when I was training for the 7 summits that he did everything he could, in a passive aggressive way, to get me to give it up.

I remember on the way to the park he wanted to stop and grab a coffee. I got more furious. Coffee? Really? We were supposed to be training, not out on a leisurely walk.

When we finally started our hike that day, I managed to blocked him out of my mind. I practiced my rest step, which I had found in Carstensz to be really hard. This mountaineering and hiking technique helps when ascending steep sloops. Essentially the rest step is a pause of motion, allowing you to rest for a short second between steps. It seems like slow walking but it's actually a kind of fast walking with rest. During the rest step, the rear leg remains vertical and fully extended, while the front leg is relaxed except when needed to adjust the balance of my body and the burden on the rear leg. Since Kilimanjaro stands at 19,340 feet or 5,985 meters, the rest step up to the summit would be needed. Steve however wasn't practicing it. He just kept moving fast again, like the previous hike, only this time he slipped and fell. I was worried as the terrain was rocky, but he said he was fine.

After two and a half hours, we made it back to the car, but I was still upset. I had wanted to hike at least another hour and not to mention, I was frustrated that it never occurred to Steve that he needed to train with his backpack weighted. It was the little things he just didn't get.

I knew I had to go to Kilimanjaro ("Kili") with him. I had to try for our relationship as husband and wife. However deep down, I did not want to. Every day we got closer to going, I became more anxious. We did not work as a team and we fought all the time. Steve never did well when he was tired, and he got flustered and tried to show off as soon as he saw someone else on the trail, especially someone of the opposite sex. It was not unlike his normal behaviour in everyday life really. I could just imagine Kilimanjaro, as sometimes there were a couple of hundred hikers trying to get to the summit.

Steve had started organizing our Kilimanjaro climb when I was preparing to leave for Carstensz. I had been happy at first, to let him do most of the arranging. It seemed important to him and I wanted to give it a chance and be supportive. Initially he seemed to be supportive or at least accepting of me climbing the 7 summits, so at the time, I just focused on the details of my first mountain.

Steve had decided we would go climb as a "new year thing". So, on January 1, 2018 we were in Africa!

The day after our arrival, two guides from the local touring company that Steve contracted met us at the hotel, gave us a brief overview of the climb schedule and then explained their services and also their tipping policies. Tipping is a very big issue in Kilimanjaro!

Mount Kilimanjaro is actually the tallest free-standing mountain in the world, and the tallest peak of Africa, but it is also a national park in Tanzania. Therefore, it attracts over twenty thousand visitors annually.

It's a busy, quite "touristy" place. Anyone in the travel industry can set you up to travel to the mountain and climb it. The campsites along the route are littered with various outfitters and guides – all local. Anyone climbing Kilimanjaro must use the service of a local guide. I say local, but I learned that the companies are actually owned by foreigners. Go figure. Our guides were from Ultimate-Kilimanjaro, a US based company, but Steve booked it through the UK. Yes, I was confused as well.

We had a guide and an assistant guide. When they led us to the bus waiting outside the hotel, there were ten other people already sitting inside; they were our porters, and a dedicated cook and a "service boy". I mused that Sandals Resorts would have called him a "butler".

Since it was January 1st and the majority of passengers were hung over from the previous night's festivities, we were told we would stop for a short breakfast along the way. It was a 3-hour bus ride to the Kilimanjaro park entrance and the Lemosho route, the trail we had decided to use. They graciously invited us to join them, and since we didn't want to wait in a hot bus, we tagged along.

Their breakfast was a beer and "barbecue". Whoa! Quite the way to start 2018! Steve sampled their "breakfast" and was not sure what part of the cow he was eating! When I called it the "stomach", Steve stopped eating. When I actually inquired what part of the cow they were consuming, our guide confirmed my suspicions.

"It's the inner part of the cow, the stomach". He continued, "I know white people don't eat that part of the cow, but for us, we eat the whole cow". I simply smiled. Steve changed colour. I remember chuckling.

Steve then reminded them I was a vegetarian. I had packed freeze-dried fruits and vegetables and dehydrated meals as a backup. Carstensz was still in my mind. However, they were not needed. Having a team of porters, which included a dedicated cook is usually part of the "Kili" experience. This part did not disappoint.

The ride to the chosen entrance gate took us past lots of farmland which surprised me. Everywhere I looked there was cattle, herds of goats and sheep. There were large spreads of agricultural land for as far as the eye could see. In Tanzania, they grow potatoes, beans, mangos, pineapples, coffee and corn among other things like ginger. It was quite spectacular.

With my backpack organized and ready, we got off the bus. Our porters helped us unload and then carried our bags to get weighed to ensure they met the maximum weight guidelines we were allowed to carry. As an aside, porters in Kilimanjaro are unionized - another indication of the level of sophistication of the climbing climate.

I had learned from Carstensz and had packed much lighter this time. This kept getting better with each mountain.

We signed in with the park ranger, with the current date, our names, profession, nationality, age and length of our stay in the park. We had to repeat this process every time we checked into a new campsite point as well as upon exiting the park. That detracted from it feeling like a wilderness adventure.

We started our day moving towards our first camp, Mti Mkubwa Camp (comes from the Swahili word meaning "big tree"), which was a hike through the park rain forest. The trails were beautifully maintained and yet natural. We saw white tailed monkeys and amazing views! This was a breathtaking part of our climb.

We climbed slowly, higher and higher... or like we learned to say in Swahili: "Pole, Pole". I learned that walking slowly, and consistently, with one foot in front of the other, was the key to reaching the top of Kilimanjaro. So much so that on Summit day, I was pleasantly surprised when I suddenly arrived at the top!

When we entered the first camp, our tent was set-up, our two duffle bags were inside our tents, and there was a toilet tent, a kitchen tent AND an eating tent. What a difference from Carstenz!! Coleman, our "service boy" who really was like a butler, informed us that as soon as we were settled, he would bring us hot water "for washing". He then asked if we would kindly go to the dining tent for some hot beverages and a snack. I kid you not – it was like being in an old English movie where you are traveling with servants. This is not your typical mountaineering expedition trip – it was a five star vacation!

Every morning, Coleman woke us up thirty minutes before bringing two bowls of hot water to the tent for washing. Then breakfast was served in a timely fashion so we could get on our way to continue the climb. The thirty minutes before washing was used to get ourselves re-packed so the porters would be ready to carry our duffle bags filled with our clothes, sleeping bags, sleeping pads, and more. I'm SO glad Carstensz was my first climb, not my second. It would have been so much harder after this "royal" treatment!

The second day took us from Mti Mkubwa directly to Shira 2 Camp. The third day we went from Shira 2 Camp that stands at 12,500 feet, and then hiked to Lava Tower Camp to 15,190 feet. We stopped there for lunch and then descended to Barranco Camp to spend the night at

13,044 feet. Climb high, sleep low was mountaineering motto for acclimatization!

The fourth day we went from Barranco Camp to Karanga Camp. After a long hike of up and down, up and down, we rested at 13,106 feet. On day five we left for Barafu Camp, or base camp at 15,331 feet.

Base camp is really more like a scene from one of those futuristic movies where there are no trees in the world and people live in makeshift homes on top lava rock. The terrain was slanted downwards which made for an interesting sleeping experience. Plus, it was bitterly cold.

When we arrived, our tents had been set. Steve had been sweating a bit that day and I had advised him to change clothes as it was getting cold. I did not want him to get cold but he ignored me. I shrugged it off, even though I was worried. A while later as we lay resting in our sleeping bags, he gestured for me to have sex, well actually more precisely, he wanted a blow job. I was speechless. Dirty, tired, and in a camp with tents all around us, he wanted sex. When I said no he got upset and couldn't understand why I was not up for it. Yes, ok, he was my husband, but climbing mountains and sex did not mesh regardless of being married to my tent mate. It was always the furthest thing from my mind. Climbing mountains is serious, it's not a vacation.

After an early dinner, we were instructed to go to sleep and Coleman would wake us up at 11:00 pm for breakfast. Yes, I said breakfast. We would start the summit climb at 12:00 midnight and needed sustenance.

Steve was still upset with me though, because after we returned to our tent to sleep, and he overheard our guides talking, he got irritated and told them rudely to be quiet and sleep. I looked at him, and simply said, "you know they are the ones guiding us to the summit, right?" And left it at that, turning on my side to sleep.

Backpacks were lightened to hold just the bare minimum, which in my case was my inReach GPS tracker, iPhone for photos, my GoPro, our passports (you never leave those) and a bag with 6 flags for photos at the peak. I also had my trekking poles, a thermos full of hot ginger tea and my water bladder with about 1.5 liters of hot water, as I wanted it available as long as I could before it froze. Plus, I had an extra two layers of clothing for the changes in temperature as we climbed.

We had been told by our guides they were only taking their water and emergency supplies, like oxygen, and one was not carrying a backpack at all. They encouraged us to not be shy about asking them to take ours. Steve's was lighter than mine; he only had water, his extra layers of clothing and his GoPro. We both had a couple of snacks, as we had cut down on the lunches that had been prepared for us.

When Iwad picked up my backpack, he said to me in a disapproving tone of voice, "This is about 7 kg with the water now."

I simply replied. "I know."

As his client, he could only respond by saying, "Well, if you need help up the mountain we can carry it."

I simply replied to his skeptical expression, which conveyed his doubt that a small woman such as myself could carry such a load to the summit, "Thank you. If I need help I will ask for it."

I didn't ask for help. I carried my backpack up and down Kilimanjaro. I felt very proud. I needed to prove to myself I could do it. In other mountains, I wouldn't have the option so I did this one unassisted. It felt good.

As we started towards the summit, I looked up and saw the familiar headlight dots moving up the mountain, showing climbers that had started ahead of us in hopes of summiting. I made a comment about it and Iwad said, "Yes, those are the very pole, pole people. We will pass them."

I didn't believe him at the time, but slowly we passed several climbers. Then more and more "pole pole", and all of a sudden, I looked up ahead and there were only a few lights moving. I looked behind me and saw a lot of lights. This fed my confidence. I believed then that we would make it.

As we slowly passed other climbers resting, I noticed that the majority of them were not carrying their backpacks. As I passed one set of climbers, I overheard a comment about a big backpack. Probably wrongly, but I immediately thought they were talking about me. It chipped away at my confidence a little, but then I kept talking to myself saying "one, two, one, two, I can do this" – and before I knew it, Iwad was telling us that we were almost at Stella Point. This point is where many climbers stop, take a photo and "call it a day", but this is not the top. It's approximately 800 meters short of the highest peak (132 meters in altitude) – Uhuru Peak.

It never occurred to me to stop at Stella Point. I honestly didn't understand why anyone would stop here. We kept going. The wind was high and the trail was thin. I started thinking we should be roped in or have crampons on our boots, or at least an ice axe with us.

Godfrey points to the left and says, "There is the glacier," as I see Steve walk a little wobbly to the left side – the side of the Glacier. I told him to please walk more to the right of Iwad. I could just imagine him slipping down the snow, towards the glacier, and with us having no ropes, nothing, it was a difficult moment.

Then all of a sudden we were at the peak. We arrived! We made it! It was windy and cold, snow was blowing and even though it was almost sunrise, we would not see the sun that morning. We started taking pictures and I still had my head light on. It felt unreal. Easy. Mixed emotions. How were we there?

Then suddenly Steve snapped me back to reality. He said he couldn't breathe. I tell Iwad to start walking back with him, to start descending as quickly as they can, as I packed up my flags and finish sending our peak location on my inReach, to record that we reached the peak and had summited. Iwad took Steve's backpack and they started descending.

A few minutes later myself and Godfrey walk swiftly to catch up to Iwad and Steve. When we reached them, Steve said he still can't breathe, so we continued walking as fast as we can. This was not the delight filled descent I had anticipated. Steve seemed to be in real distress.

Descending was not easy. When we passed Stella Point I noticed many climbers were taking pictures, others were sitting and resting. We took a different path – it was all downwards.

After a few more minutes, I looked on my altimeter watch and knew we were already a couple of hundred feet lower in altitude. I looked at Steve's face and it seemed purple. Just then I noticed the baklava he was wearing seemed to be choking him. I told him to take it off. Once he did, I noticed a deep crease that ran from his forehead to his chin. The baklava was choking him! After a few moments he said, "That feels better." I was so relieved, but admittedly, I rolled my eyes in silence.

We passed a couple of people being helped with oxygen by their guides. Another individual was being carried along by two other men. Even though this climb felt 'touristy', it was clear that those who were ill prepared, were paying the price.

We arrived back at base camp at about 8:45 am. Our porters cheered for us. We had done it! Coleman had four glasses of mango juice and four chairs waiting for us. We celebrated. It was nice. For a brief moment I was happy to be there, with Steve, and having summited my second mountain.

We were told to rest until 11:00 am and then be packed by 11:30 am. At this point we would be served lunch so we could continue our descent to Mweka Camp, approximately 9,000 feet lower. This is where we would spend the last night of our Kilimanjaro climb, before descending the rest of the way down the following morning and exiting the park at the Mweka park gate before noon the following day.

During the descent, Steve kept racing down, even though the guides kept asking him to slow down because the terrain was uneven, slippery and rocky in some areas. But he just wanted to get to camp and lay down he later disclosed. He told me this after I complained to him that he didn't even wait or turned around when I slipped and fell and injured my knee. Like during our training hikes at home, we were not a team, and Steve could not care less about me, or how my knee was hurting me.

Taking six days to climb and 24 hours to descend worked the front muscles of my legs; muscles I have to be honest, I had never felt so vividly. I clearly needed to work out more for descending mountains.

Was the climb challenging? It was.

Did I find it hard? Not really.

Did I enjoy it? No.

During our descent to Mweka, I had noticed metal contraptions scattered along the side the trail. They were stretchers, with two front heavy-duty tires, with super tire shocks. I first noticed just a couple of them, but then a few feet further down, I noticed many more. They were stretchers for injured climbers and porters. We didn't see them on the way up because now we were descending Kilimanjaro on a different route to help control climber traffic flow!

The stats were startling. It was reported that yearly approximately 1,000 people get evacuated from Kilimanjaro. Approximately 10 deaths were reported for that same time frame, but it's believed that those numbers are at least 3 to 4 times higher.

I believe it. I understand the lure of climbing a mountain and have experienced the drunken, happy feeling one feels when you reach the Summit. It truly is intoxicating! But I also understand the hard work it takes to train, the safety issues that need to be respected and the commitment required to persevere. Kilimanjaro is a huge tourist destination that attracts an enormous amount of people, including many that are ill prepared for the climb that there were bound to be accidents.

When we arrived at Mweka Camp, I was exhausted. I had been awake and moving for about 16 hours. We had climbed to 5,585 meters and then descended to about 3,100 meters. My relationship with Steve had preoccupied my mind.

After setting up my sleeping bag and his, we rested for a few moments until Coleman came to announce dinner. We reluctantly went to eat. I just wanted to rest and be, but Coleman tells us to please stay seated after dinner as they had a surprise planned. We stayed.

The surprise was a baked cake, congratulating us on the successful climb. I asked the cook how he did it. He baked a cake, with a vanilla ganache topping, in a one burner camping stove. He even wrote our names and had it decorated. I can't even do that in my professional stove at home. It was amazing! Steve and I had a slice each and then we had Coleman cut a slice for the rest of the porters and team.

The next day we continued our descent and exited the park.

CHAPTER 8
ELBRUS

This was the beginning of several hard choices I would have to make for my personal mental health, choices about what my life would look like from here on. Sometimes it still seems like this was also the beginning of the end of my marriage, even though I know it was not.

The beginning of that end was actually in April 2009. This climb however, was when I started to heal and gained the courage to finally leave Steve and end my marriage of twenty-two years.

A week before I was scheduled to leave for Elbrus, Steve flew to Barcelona to get surgery to change his natural hazel eye colour to blue. He paid over eleven thousand euros to the only clinic he told me, in the world that does this surgery. The procedure would be done using laser.

I didn't understand why he wanted to do this. His reasoning was that he had always wanted blue eyes, but also because I was spending money to go climbing so he was going to do this. If I cancelled my climb, he would cancel his trip.

Needless to say, Steve went to Barcelona for a week to do this surgery and arrived back in Toronto the day I left for Russia. I don't know if he went to Barcelona alone, I don't think he did, but I can tell you that today, his eyes are still hazel.

I left Toronto on Friday, July 20th in the early evening. I was going to be climbing Elbrus alone, without my friend Emmanuel.

That first day of long flights was a necessary part of this adventure. I arrived at Moscow Airport late Saturday afternoon, July 21st and instantly marveled at the sight of Russia. It didn't look at all like it's portrayed in the movies. It looked like any other country. Having said that, the people did seem different. They didn't smile a lot. They were polite and did their jobs, but there were no smiles offered.

As I met up with my group, I was relieved that everyone seemed nice. This would make it easier because as part of these adventures, you had to make friends with and rely on all sorts of people.

I was happy to see two other females in the group in addition to our guide Carole. She and her husband Vern Tejas were highly experienced and ranked among the best in mountaineering circles. Yet they exuded politeness and happiness – like they really liked their jobs.

The hotel was OK. It has a bed and a bathroom; just a functional space. No smiles there either.

By Sunday, July 22nd, jetlag was affecting me (heavy sigh). I had had a very hard time sleeping beyond the hour I slept around 11:30 pm local time. I did manage to fall asleep again around 3:30 am but it was not a deep sleep, really just resting in a semi aware state.

Still, I was excited to be there. I was actually in Russia! The day was spent touring Moscow: Red Square, the Kremlin, and the cemetery where politicians and famous Russian socialites are buried. I found the tombstones fascinating and disturbing, but also quite pretentious. Statues served as headstones for the deceased, including people like Boris Yeltsin, whose headstone was an abstract piece of art.

The architecture was wonderful and fascinating. The details that showed Persian, Portuguese and even Spanish influences were wonderful to see. The city was extremely clean, perhaps the cleanest city I have ever visited. Certainly, Moscow puts to shame the dirty, smelling streets of New York City.

I also enjoyed seeing the changing of the guard, an English monarchy influence. But still, the lack of smiles of Russian residents was something that I kept noticing. There was an emptiness to it. Though never rude to anyone, their presence was never warm, inviting or happy. It seemed strange to me. Now that I look back, it was actually a perfect metaphor for my marriage.

Common belief is that if you smile at another person, and you are being polite and cheerful, it will evoke similar feelings in return. Not there. I tried, but to no avail. No response. None.

Our team of fellow climbers were a wonderful group. It was easy to bond with them. Our Alpine Ascents guides, Carole and Vern, were not only professional, but warm, caring and excellent hosts and guides. They shared not only their guidance and leadership, but their friendship and love for mountaineering.

I was privileged to learn from Carole that she and Vern actually got married on the summit of Vinson Massif in Antarctica. Vern had proposed on their way to the summit. They both were climbing alone, roped together, and he shouted down to her, "So, do you want to get married?" and Carole simply answering back, "Sure!" Vern was not a man to wait to get things done so when he saw another guide he knew that was licensed to officiate marriages on his way down from the summit with a client, he immediately asked if he would marry him and Carole.

And so it was, this guide with the client in tow, turned around and married Vern and Carole at the top of the Summit. Both bride and groom wore climate warming outfits, with ropes and carabiners hanging from their harnesses. It was a true mountain top marriage!

That was over ten years ago, but as Carole told the romantic story, I could still see the love reflected in her eyes. Not many people can say they got proposed to and married in Antarctica, on the highest mountain of that continent! Priceless.

For what was our day four, I once again only managed to sleep an hour before laying wide awake at 1:30 am. I had to get up at 5:00 am, shower and get ready, then check out of the hotel and meet my group in the hotel lobby at 5:50 am to head to the airport. Somehow I made it.

I always have a hard time sleeping when I am stressed, sad, heartbroken and alone. The anguish of my personal life was germinating in my soul and it was affecting me physically, but I kept going.

From Moscow, we headed to Mineralyne Vody, on our way to Elbrus, the highest peak in Europe. The flight took about two hours, followed by a three hour bus ride.

Shortly after we landed, I encountered my first real test. "Ok team!" Vern stated, "We have about a kilometre to walk over to where our ride is. Put your duffels on your back and carry your backpacks on the front."

"Easy. No really Ema, easy" I desperately told myself as I tried to talk myself into it. I was quite nervous. The experience on Mount Rainier and the heavy loads had my heart racing so fast I thought it might suffocate me. It threaten to come up my throat and vomit out.

Even with cutting down my gear, my duffel still weighed 55 pounds! Ten of my twelve teammates were guys, and fortunately one of them helped me secure one of my straps that kept sliding down my arm. I walked awkwardly forward, mainly because the duffel bag was three quarters my size. Despite the weight, it didn't bother me much. "I can do this" I kept silently telling myself as I put one foot in front of the other. After about only one hundred meters we arrived at our location. I was happy! Phew. Test one – check. Vern had just freaked us out on purpose.

After driving for a few minutes, we stopped for lunch and the group had chicken, lamb and beef. Myself, I had some salad, grilled vegetables, fresh bread with butter and tea. I learned that this part of Russia enjoys many Persian influences and the restaurant we ate lunch at reflected it.

We arrived in Tersol after a three hour bus ride. We were there at last! Tersol was a small ski town at the base of Mount Elbrus. The lodge where we stayed, was not luxurious, but clean and we were the only residents. We were a group of fifteen in total. Vern and Carole introduced us to the two Angelas, who owned the property and would take care of us during our stay. The Angela duo did smile.

The following day, day five of our itinerary, was our first acclimatization day. We hiked for about five to six hours. We hiked up tall grass and a steep hill towards the Observatory.

It was on this day that Vern and Carole taught us about pressure breathing. Some of my teammates seemed to have theirs already down pat, but I always felt out of breath. When I learned this style of breathing at Mount Rainier, I found it complicated. It made me lightheaded and even more short of breath. Breathing should not be this complicated! With the help of Vern and Carole, I learned it wasn't. Their method was to blow the stale air out of your lungs by filling your mouth with air until you get cheeks like a chipmunk, and then blow it out like you are exasperated with someone. Bingo! That felt great!

On day six we climbed a different side of the valley. When we were very close to the Georgian border, most of the team joked about crossing the border illegally; like attempting to climb Elbrus was not dangerous enough! Did we really need the prospect of getting shot or detained either by Georgian authorities or the Russia police to be added to the mix?! Fortunately, no casualties to report.

Each day we climbed up to more than 10,000 feet in altitude. We learned to pace ourselves and I kept practicing my new breathing technique. Both days we saw Mount Elbrus towering over the valley. Mount Elbrus is an extinct volcano with two cones, and it stands at 5,642 m or 18,510 ft. Since Russian became part of Europe, it's officially the tallest peak in Europe, and therefore part of the 7 Summits. When Russia was part of the USSR, Europe's highest peak was Mount Blanc.

On day seven, we repack our duffel bags. We left whatever wasn't a necessity on the mountain in our second small duffle bag and locked it. It was stored for us in a room until our descent from the mountain.

We loaded the van with our duffel bags, backpacks and forty litres of water; four bottles of five litres each per climber. We were then driven to the tram. There was no turning back and I was nervous. Again.

Base camp at Mount Elbrus was a very dirty place. Let me explain. There was garbage everywhere. The toilets were three walls and a door, with a hole in the bottom. Each time someone used these 'facilities', urine and feces would just free fall in the air and land on the rocks that lay underneath.

Our accommodation was one of the nicer ones. Inside it was hostel style; eight of us shared one room, sleeping on four pairs of bunk beds. The staff was constantly washing the floors. We kept our hiking boots contained to a designated area but despite this and their efforts, it was hard to keep it clean inside when no one cleans outside.

We were not there for a vacation so I set aside my evaluation of the surroundings and concentrated on training as directed. Vern and Carole didn't let us waste any time. Right after lunch we did a short hike on the glacier. They took the opportunity to teach and review hiking roped up as a group. In mountaineering, we'll rope up with others for safety and travel as a team when tackling challenging terrain such as crossing a glacier or ascending a steep snow slope on your way to the summit and back. If someone slips on a slope or falls into a crevasse, others on the team self-arrest and act as the human anchor to stop the fall. Team members then work together to rescue the fallen climber . This exercise was great to practice.

The following day we took a longer hike, in altitude. We climbed up to the Pastukhov Rocks area, even though on summit day, we would take the "Cat" up to this point and start our accent from there. Caterpillar machines (often called the "Cat") were available to take climbers up the mountain. We used them. This day we also used our crampons for the first time. We got them properly fitted to our boots and I was pleased that Vern helped fit mine flawlessly to my Sportiva Spantik boots. His experienced hands helped me with a couple of adjustments (stretching and bending).

During that training walk we gained about fifteen thousand feet in altitude. We were getting acclimatized with each hike.

Later in the afternoon, we reviewed the intricacies of anchor building. There were crevasses on the glacier and being armed with more knowledge and skills is nothing but a benefit.

Our eighth day, July 28th, was supposed to be a rest day, as the following day we would attempt to summit the tallest peak in Europe. However, as athletes we couldn't just laze around all day, we decided to practice our ice axe skills. These skills are crucial for self-confidence and readiness in emergencies, in case of an accidental fall or slip.

We spend a couple of hours in the morning practicing just that. We replicated, on purpose, several ways we could fall and how to use our ice axe self-arrest, to stop us from sliding down the glacier, away from the possible reach of our teammates. This was a potential lifesaving maneuver. Very important.

Although we did not anticipate traversing over any crevasses during our summit accent, Vern and Carole set up a couple of stations for self-extraction, out of a crevasse, so we could refresh the theory and practice the skill for other mountains. Learning from the man that currently holds the title of 70 Summits, meaning, he has climbed all 7 Summits, ten times each, was a privilege.

After that, it was a rest day. Vern had been looking at the blowing snow at the top of Elbrus and watching the weather. He had estimated the day after would be our summit day.

Rest was not easy. Several of our teammates were suffering from intestinal problems and lots of trips to the "facilities" were necessary. We all worried about what we were eating. Being a vegetarian is still tricky when travelling, well climbing. Only having access to specific supplies makes it that much harder, so I am almost more limited than others.

Intestinal problems is what nightmares are made of for mountaineers. The last thing one needs on summit day is a bathroom due to diarrhea or vomiting.

My summit day outfit is customary. I always pack it separately from other clothes in my duffle bags. Like your "Sunday best" expression, your "summit day outfit" is also an expression when climbing mountains. We each took turns, for privacy, during the afternoon to put on our summit day clothes and get our backpacks ready.

On Sunday, July 29th, 2018 our team "Putin on the Ritz", named this after Vern's insistence we come up with a team name, set our alarms for a 2:00 am breakfast. On this ninth day of our adventure, I, like several of my teammates, was already up. Vern turned on the electrical kettle for hot water, to warm our first batch of water bottles, and then we were ready to go.

Our plan had been to be ready and mobile at 3:00 am and be by the "cats" to put our crampons on at 3:30 am. And that's what we did. Our two "snow cats" quickly filled with our equipment as our large group awkwardly got on board. We sat excited, anticipating what was to come and we held on tight as the "snow cats" brought us up the mountain, to just past the Provesky Rocks on Mount Elbrus. Then we all jumped off. Our summit push had begun.

We removed our down jackets because it was important to start cold I learned. I followed Vern's advice about this for the rest of the peaks. Vern had advised that we should start cold because our bodies heat up fast once we start moving. We put on our snow googles next, with our face buffs securely tucked underneath its strap so not to leave any of our face exposed. My buff had a Canadian flag print, demonstrating how proud I am to be Canadian!

It was windy and cold as we started out. We all knew that as we gained altitude, the temperature would decrease and the winds would increase. The clear blue skies we had been seeing the previous days as we glanced up the mountain from base camp were merely a rouse. Clearly, this was NOT going to be easy.

The previous day, when we were informed by Vern that we would attempt our summit, it was with the expectation the weather would be similar to the previous day. The report from climbers that had reached the Summit was that they had to literally "crawl" to the Peak. I had visualized the "crawling" action myself and yet only half believed Vern when he told us. I thought he was exaggerating. In a few short hours, I learned first-hand, that "crawling" was the right verb. A daunting exercise; but the only way.

With our backpacks securely buckled on our backs, our headlamps turned on, we got to business. We ensured our ice axe was deployable - this can be done in different ways, but I usually put mine in between my back and by backpack. I adjusted both my trekking poles at the appropriate climbing length. These were two skills I learned and reviewed until they became second nature as I climbed.

In a single file, one step at a time, practicing both our rest-step and pressure breathing, we started to climb. I concentrated on both, and at the same time, ensured each of my steps were careful ones so as to not get my crampons tangled on each other. I concentrated on my rhythm and nothing else.

"One, two, whooof.... one, two, whooof..."

I know to others looking at us from below or even from behind, we looked like fireflies slowly moving up the mountain with only the light from our headlamps visible. It's a common site on summit day in every mountain. Fireflies in a string, moving upward in the extreme cold and wind.

When daylight was breaking and we reached our first stop, Vern directed us. He reminded us, "Keep warm people." "Ten minute break." "Remember to pee, drink and eat – in that order." "You do not want to be caught with your pants down when we are ready to go!" His sense of humour would lift our spirits. His constant advice was welcomed and I recalled it on all my other climbs.

The first rest stop was by a broken down, red, snow caterpillar, that seemed a fixture on the ridge. I doubted it would ever be removed, it's just another piece of "garbage" on Elbrus.

Modesty in the mountain does not exist. It was always my greatest fear but one I soon became immune to. I learned to accept my basic nature needs, and thankfully, learned that everyone is very respectful when you need to go.

"Two minutes people!" Vern commanded and we knew it was time to wrap it up and get going. We all responded as quickly as possible.

We continued our ascent as the sun slowly slid up past the fluffy white clouds, painting a golden halo around them. It rose to set its place against the blue sky. For a brief moment, both sun and moon shared the same space. It's so magical what God creates. And from this vantage point, even more so.

Anatoli, the "official" mountain photographer was going around from group to group, capturing special moments, which he would then sell to us in a couple of days. He climbed the mountain every day. Vern told us at one point to simply pull our buffs down for a brief smile into Anatoli's camera as we pass him. We did. It recorded our red faces out from under our buffs.

Our second break was on the vertical face of the mountain, just off the narrow trekking path. As we followed our break routine, I tried not to think of the height we were at or consider that one slip would have any one of us demonstrating our ice axe arrest techniques. Better not to think of that possibility. None of us wanted to practice that. I tried not to look back because of my fear of heights and instead simply told myself I was on solid footing. It helped.

As we continued in single file, we came upon another group, which after a few moments, our guides and theirs negotiated our passing ahead of them. All of our group secretly felt good about this maneuver. We seemed to be moving at a decent pace!

I could see we were entering the saddle. The saddle is termed as such because it's a dip between both mountain peaks, resembling an actual saddle.

While in the saddle, the wind was not as prevalent and I foolishly thought that Vern was exaggerating about the wind speed we were to expect. I learned quickly never to doubt Vern!

As I looked ahead I could see blowing snow creating dust clouds against and around other fellow climbers already at the base of the saddle and making their way up the other side towards the Summit. The brief stillness we felt was much like the proverbial "calm before the storm".

As we reached the saddle base, the wind demonstrated its superiority. It pushed us like a bully, demanding we pushed back and fight to keep ourselves vertical.

Vern commanded and guided us efficiently to get our down jackets on. We needed to pee, drink and eat like on any other break, plus we needed to put our harnesses on. We secured all our backpacks and trekking poles in a pile and left them behind before our final push. This was both to facilitate our final push up to the Summit, but also to save space – there was not much room up there!

Our guides helped us get our harnesses on, without taking our crampons off. As Irina and "Jason" (not his real name but nicknamed by us because of his white face mask) helped us, I made a mental note to get a better harness for my future climbs. Then we were off, for the final leg.

Shortly after, we were feeling the wind's defiant tease to "take him on" with only our ice axe in hand as if we could threaten the wind to 'back off'. Just as we clipped on the static line, the wind retreated, teasing, giving us a false sense of hope. Then it came gusting back against us with speeds of about 50 km an hour. At moments the wind took a deep breath and exhaled ice pellets that hit our faces and bodies, making demanding threats against us. I had never experienced wind like this. Truly, if we broke our attention from it, it would and could toss us into the abyss. I briefly wondered if this is what Denali or Vinson would feel like, but I didn't have much time to ponder this thought as all my energy was spent concentrating on each step, bracing myself with my ice axe and also guiding my reach on the fixed rope.

Suddenly it dawned on me, we were "crawling" up to the Peak. The roar of the wind, the sting of the ice pallets on the face, and the concentration required, were all very real. We were indeed crawling to the top.

Then as we left the fixed rope section, we continued slowly, hunched down, up the glacier ridge towards the summit point. It was in sight and that encouraged us but we all moved very slowly and carefully. Even though the wind had given up throwing snow dust at us, it continued to push us defiantly.

And then suddenly – we were there! We were at the top of Mount Elbrus! We did it! I did it! The Summit space was maybe a 10×12 foot small, cramped space. Our group alone filled it, as others compete to share the area.

At the same time, I realized and felt like the wind was going to blow me away. This was not a good feeling; despite the relief at being successful, I still needed to concentrate.

I hunched down and secured my ice axe on its floor. I started to pull out my first flag, the Portuguese and Canada flags I had sewn together, and realized the wind was blowing it like an out of control boat sail. Another climber saw me struggle and helped me hold an end, while Andrey took a picture.

I knew it would not be possible to take pictures of all my flags: the Language Marketplace flag, the Peaks for Change flag, CAMH, and why I climb. I also realized that I would not be able to take a picture of my #JesusRocks flag that I hand painted in Rainier. My heart tugs in sadness.

I quickly stuffed the flag into my jacket and tried to hold up my "Julia and Ethan" flag, for my grandkids. They're my "Prozac" my psychiatrist once told me, when she described how my eyes shine when I talk about them. Unfortunately, the wind crumples it in response as Andrey snaps a quick picture for me. This was the worst picture.

I then joined the rest of the group for a group summit photo and just like that, it was over.

Done.

It reminds me of a wedding. It takes so much time, effort and preparation and you look forward to it with great anticipation, but then it's over so quickly. On that day, there was no time to savor the moment. It was time to move on. Others were waiting to take our place and wanted us to move along. I did however have time to take a deep breath and look around in a 360 degree motion, memorizing the true beauty that scourged us below. Peaks adoring the horizon around us, like a crown, as we stood at the top of Europe.

It was here that I realized God had me in a journey, one to make my faith stronger. By trusting and believing whole heartily in Him, that He would show me that my pain would subside and give me purpose.

CHAPTER 9
VINSON MASSIF

Emmanuel climbed and summited Vinson Massif with me.

Climbing Mount Vinson and going to Antarctica was nerve racking. I felt there was a lot riding on the success of the expedition, and not just monetary.

Climbing Mount Vinson is the most expensive of the 7 Summits, after Everest. The remoteness of Antarctica and the time constraint on being able to access the mountain plays a huge role in the cost. There is a short season to climb Vinson, from late November to mid-January.

I was interviewed, did mandatory winter climbing and crevasse rescue training with Leo in Quebec, this time without breaking any ribs or anything.

We were one of the first groups of the season. We travelled with and had chosen ALE (Antarctic Logistics & Expeditions) as our expedition guiding company as ALE is the only operator with flights to access Vinson. ALE has operated continuously in Antarctica since 1987. They were the first land-based tour operator using wheeled aircraft on blue-ice runways. They have safely executed hundreds of roundtrip intercontinental flights from Chile to the interior of Antarctica and have supported virtually every private expedition that has skied, flown or driven across Antarctica. The extra few hundred dollars in cost was worth it.

Packed, and ready to go, we left Toronto on November 13, 2018. I had expected Emmanuel to arrive late at Pearson, like when we climbed Carstensz, but to my surprised he had beaten me to the airport. He had partied too much the night before though as it had been his birthday and was still in party mode come flight time.

We went a whole week ahead to Punta Arenas to explore Patagonia. I had packed two bags; one for exploring Patagonia and one, my North Face yellow duffle, ready for Union Glacier full of every item on Antarctic Logistics & Expeditions list and weighing in under 55 pounds. It had been just over a year since I climbed my first mountain, Carstensz Pyramid, and I was so scared.

We flew from Toronto to Santiago, Chile on Air Canada, then we transferred planes to Punta Arenas. We had departed Toronto at 9:10 pm the previous night. It was a long flight.

When I woke up, the sky looked clear. In my confusion of either waking up on the plane or my excitement of going to Antarctica, I unbuckled my seat belt, kneeled on my still fully extended bed like a child jumping in bed, and look at the beautiful scenery, confusing the clouds as snow. When I ask the flight attendant if it was snow below, she amusingly smiled and said, "snow, no, it looks that way because of the auto blinders in the windows, but it's 30 degrees down there, there is no snow." "Oh" I said and smiled and thinking to myself, oh yes, there is lots of snow where I am going.

Emmanuel had listened to this exchange. As I retracted my seat to a sitting position getting ready for breakfast a few moments later, I looked again out the window and could see mountains. Emmanuel said from his seat, "It's Aconcagua!". I saw him smiling as I look towards him, nodding his head in confirmation. As I looked back outside, my heart raced a little faster looking at the mountain. I already had Aconcagua booked and would be climbing it on my own. I took a deep breath and thought, first things first, right now we were doing Vinson. I shook the thoughts and feeling away. At this time, I was climbing Vinson Massif with my best friend.

The first morning in Punta Arenas I got up early, with the sunrise at 4:30 am local time. After some time, I went out to look around the city. I saw a dog in the back of a pickup truck patiently waiting and thought of my dog Daisy back home. I missed her. As I walked towards the water, downtown, I saw the Portuguese flag on a gorgeous building that was now a bar and restaurant. I thought with a smile how the Portuguese were everywhere.

Around mid-morning we had a gear check with Robert Anderson, from ALE. Robert had also picked us up from the airport the day before. At the time, neither myself nor Emmanuel realized the legend and honour of having Robert as our liaison representative for ALE that season. We didn't find out until a few days later, when we met more members of our team. Robert "Madds" Anderson is an author, speaker, creative director and mountaineer who has climbed the 7 Summits solo. Above it all, I found he was a man that exemplifies humility. It awed me. I knew from meeting him, that this trip would be a great learning experience for me.

During our gear check Robert patiently went through some housekeeping rules and provided valuable advice for our time in Vinson. As a result of this advice, Emmanuel reluctantly had to go buy another pair of gloves. He had argued he didn't need them, and in the end he was right, but certain gear is mandatory when temperatures can reach -50 degrees Celsius. The gloves were important and Robert did not budge on the requirement.

That afternoon we went to buy Emmanuel gloves, and while out, we made plans to go explore Patagonia and hike Torres del Paine. We rented a car and made hotel reservations. We also walked to the monument of Fernão de Magalhães, the Portuguese explorer, and posed for a picture by the foot. Other tourists were kissing his foot, as legend has it that if you kiss the foot, you will surely come back to Punta Arenas. But legends aside, I am somewhat a germaphobe, so posing was enough for me. And since I am not superstitious, I am hoping I will return to

Punta Arenas again. The following day we went to see penguins.

After, we left Punta Arenas, we spent a couple of days in Patagonia. Patagonia is a region encompassing the vast southernmost tip of South America, shared by Argentina and Chile, with the Andes Mountains as its dividing line. We hiked Torres del Paine; three hours up, and one hour thirty minutes down. Totally worth it. Hiking Torres del Paine, which is part of the famous W-Trek, was an incredible experience. The majestic beauty of valleys, views of snow topped peaks, glacier lakes, gorgeous rock formations and of course the fresh air was an indescribable experience that was the perfect prelude to Vinson.

I was told approximately 275,000 visitors a year visit the area. Compare that to the population of only 170,000, you can conclude that it was a busy trail. And not everyone was a hiker. I distinctively remember Emmanuel's irritation seeing a young woman in designer sandals, walking gingerly on the loose rocks as we hiked towards the top and end of the trail.

On the other side of the "W" was great hiking that led to a gorgeous iceberg. I had never seen an iceberg. Almost at the end of the trail, where we would have a great view of the iceberg, we came across a solo traveler. She asked us in French if we spoke French, as she seemed a little lost. Emmanuel of course responded. It took at least fifteen minutes before Emmanuel realized I was there waiting, in the cold wind, as he flirted with this girl. I knew it was in his nature to flirt but I love him anyways and feel very blessed to have him as my best friend. At the time I recalled thinking there must be something about me and men. I felt invisible as soon as another female was around. Reflecting since, I am sure it was just PTSD because of Steve.

Back in Punta Arenas I sat alone, anxious, inside the hotel restaurant Rey Don Philippe, looking out into the street. It was sunny, but the wind was blowing. It was always windy and cold there, and it was summer. We learned no one used an umbrella when it rained because the wind would destroy them. Emmanuel spent all the time he could in his room, sleeping. He knew that sharing a tent is not easy. I secretly envied him. I just couldn't do it. I was so restless.

ALE transport service came to pick up our duffels a couple of hours later. I felt excited but knew I still needed to decide if I wanted to pack the running shoes I was wearing that morning. I had started to feel a little of out of place always wearing my Valentino blue boots, boots I had been wearing for the past 4 or 5 days even when going out to eat and sightseeing, so had put on my runners. Even now I still don't understand why anyone wears hiking shoes when not hiking or climbing. Anyway, that morning I gave in, since technically our expedition was about to start, and decided not to pack my running shoes. I wish I had.

My throat was hurting a little that morning and thought Steve's cold may have finally caught up to me. I was hoping I would be ok in Antarctica because I imagined it would not be good being sick there. I knew I could take meds while there, but it would not be ideal. I had been taking lots of Vitamin C, actually downing it, and took some more as we waited to leave.

After our luggage was picked up around 11:00 am, we had a group lunch at 12:30 pm where we met some of the other people that would be climbing with us.

We had an information session at the ALE office at 4:00 pm, where we also picked up our boarding passes for the next days' flight to Antarctica. The boarding passes were the best, they had a penguin on them.

Robert Anderson, our local ALE representative, gave us an overview presentation of what to expect in Antarctica. There were several groups present including those climbing Vinson, guests going to visit the Emperor Penguins, those skiing the last degree, those going on solo expeditions to the South Pole, and even a couple with a solar powered car, going across Antarctica. The car had been printed using a 3D printer. I kid you not.

During the ALE briefing I also met Sherpa Lakpa Rita, who was going to be one of our guides. Lakpa became the first Sherpa to climb the 7 Summits, including climbing Everest seventeen times. I was a little starstruck I have to admit.

On schedule the next morning, November 26, we went to the airport and boarded the Ilyushin. The Ilyushin Il-76 was a Russian, multi-purpose four-engine plane that was first intended as a commercial freighter in 1967. It was designed to deliver heavy machinery to remote, poorly served areas. Military versions of the Il-76 have been widely used in Europe, Asia and Africa.

ALE leased one of these planes for the season. The plane came with its own Russian crew. It was modified inside with some seats and, since there were no windows, a large screen TV was installed at the front of the plane so passengers could watch the plane being guided on the runway, take off and land. The TV received the feed from a camera outside the front of the plane.

ALE also had its own flight attendant on every flight to give us earplugs, a beverage or two and a couple of snacks.

The Ilyushin takes enough fuel for a return trip from Punta Arenas to Union Glacier.

I couldn't believe my luck! I got to sit beside Lakpa. It was as exciting to me at that moment, as if it had been Bon Jovi.

When we arrived at Union Glacier, the plane landed on a blue ice runway and even though the Ilyushin did not have any trouble stopping, us passengers felt somewhat out of place as we slipped and slid on the ice. It was cold and windy but our excitement at arriving was great. We posed for several pictures in front of the plane before we boarded the trucks taking us to Union Glacier's camp.

I was in Antarctica! It was cold! It was like being in a place out of this world. I remember feeling giddy, elated and happy. Emmanuel smiled and I'm sure he was feeling the same way.

The ride from the runway to the camp was about 25 minutes, even though the distance was only about 5-6 kilometers. We were in these souped up Ford vehicles, with monster winter tires.

When we reach Union Glacier, we were given a tour of the camp, the facilities, and given a rundown of the do's and do not's in the bathrooms. Did I mention it was cold?

The views all around me were so clear and clean, it was as if I was wearing prescription sunglasses that I had to keep reminding myself not to take off. The snow was so clear and bright it could blind you. I remember Vern in Elbrus saying if we took our sunglasses off, our eyes would hurt so much, as it would feel like we had sandpaper inside our eyeballs. I never tried to prove his theory wrong or right, throughout any of the mountains covered in snow.

We were assigned a tent. The tents were a clamshell shape, with carpet on the floor and cots. There was a folding table in between our cots. Emmanuel and I shared a tent. Our bags were delivered by skidoo! Union Glacier was basically a resort on ice!

After settling into our tents, we were invited to the communal dining tent. ALE does not serve your average cafeteria food! There were vegan and gluten free choices, fresh baked goods and meals made fresh for breakfast, lunch and dinner, and of course mid-morning and afternoon snacks! Hot water, tea and coffee was always available and during meals white and red wine.

Union Glacier was our first clue that climbing Mount Vinson was not going to be your average Summit attempt. At least not when ALE was your expedition services guide. It spoiled me.

On our first day in Antarctica, after dinner at Union Glacier, there had been talk about the possibility of having us flown to base camp that evening. There was even a person from ALE walking around with a flight scheduled. I have to mentioned that in Antarctica, it takes about two months for the sun to rise (August through October) and then it stays daylight from October through March. Then it takes another two months for the sun to set (March through May). Finally, it stays well below the horizon from May through August when Antarctica is in complete darkness. We didn't end up leaving that evening as the weather did not co-operate. We spent the night at Union Glacier in our clamshell resort room.

The next morning, on November 27 after breakfast, we boarded one of the twin otter planes operated by Ken Borek Air, a Calgary based airline. They were the company hired by ALE to fly the season in Antarctica. Emmanuel and I were on the first flight. Lakpa and Sebastian, one of the guides, also flew with us to base camp as we were the first group of the season.

All of ALE guides are ultra-qualified and are assigned a rotation schedule of working as guides and rangers. The rangers in Vinson are ALE guides who are also available to assist other climbers with their expeditions in case of an emergency.

Our flight to base camp was about 20 minutes, and all we could see out the frosted windows was snow-covered peaks. Of course, we were in Antarctica.

When we landed, we were greeted by a smiling, happy head guide named Tre-C (pronounced Tracy). She knew our names, greeted us all like old friends and then proceeded to give us the most important tour; how to pee in Antarctica.

Number "2" is flown out of Antarctica, back to Chile, but "pee" remains in Antarctica as per the Antarctic Treaty. The Antarctic Treaty is an environmental protocol with set guidelines to deal with waste disposal and management, which essentially directs that "as far as practicable so as to minimize impacts on the Antarctic environment and to minimize interference with the natural values of Antarctica".

Our sleeping quarters at base camp were huge dome shape tents that could accommodated at least 4 people inside each. I could even stand inside them. Yes, I am a short person but even Emmanuel, after refuting my comment saying he could "not relate", was also able to stand. He said," I stand corrected, I CAN relate," after I politely had asked him to stand in the middle of the tent himself, and he obliged cynically. I had gone directly into our tent after our tour of base camp, while he had gone to socialize (and probably flirt). Both of us had our own single mattress to lay our sleeping bags on. The entire tent was laid on top of plywood boards to separate direct contact between the snow and the tent floor.

Our group tent, which was also ALE's base camp office and kitchen, was heated. It had chairs and tables for all of us to hang out at, hot water at our disposal for tea, coffee, and hot chocolate. Breakfast, lunch, and dinner were served here, along with an array of soft drinks, beer, red and white wine, as well as champagne for celebrations and sangria for treats. This was just for ALE's clients.

At base camp, there were groups from other different expedition companies. They set-up their own tents, including their own kitchen and dining tents, etc.

I realized there was an argument to be made for those that call themselves "purists", but this was the best way to experience the mountains and true mountaineering. The comforts and attention to detail and may I venture to say, the touch of luxury (in the mountaineering realm) that ALE provides in Vinson is incredible.

In Everest, no one complains when using the services of Sherpas, or in Kilimanjaro using porters. Well, in Vinson, I am of the opinion that one should climb using ALE. Why can't one enjoy climbing the tallest mountain in Antarctica in more comfort? I saw no reason and still don't.

We still carried our own personal equipment to the other two camps. We still climbed up the same fixed rope from low to high camp. We still 'trekked' the same distance from high camp to the Summit. But we enjoyed a little more comfort. I know some of the other mountaineering companies and they are wonderful of course, but I am just saying, ALE has the right idea. I wanted to climb the 7 Summits and did not see any reason why I couldn't enjoy it as much as possible. After all isn't "mountaineering" just the act of climbing mountains? Anyway, I digress.

The next day, on November 28th, 2018, our three assigned guides, Lakpa, Seba and Tre-C divided our team of nine, into three rope teams, randomly selected. Each rope team had three climbers and one guide. At all times when outside the camp areas, we were roped in together, because of the existence of crevasses.

Myself, Emmanuel and Christian, a fellow mountaineer from France, were in Seba's rope team.

On Lakpa's team were David, Matt, and Nicolas, then Tre-C had Jenny, her husband Matt and Steve (no relation to my ex-husband). This last team became the British connection rope team!

We practiced putting our crampons on. And we went for a small acclimatization hike, training, to get used to being roped in, the team's pace, the weather and of course ensuring our crampons were working well on our boots and confirming our clothing layering system was working for us. This is a common practice in all mountains.

The next day, we learned the weather reports were not favourable for the next few days, so our guides explained to us that we would continue to acclimatize in base camp.

However, to keep us "prepared", we got a lesson on how to rig and attach the sleds to our backpacks. We would use the sleds to take supplies to low camp. In each rope team, only three sleds would be used, meaning the last person on the rope team would not have a sled.

November 30th, 2018, we were still hanging out at base camp and we got our food planned for when we started to move to the low and high camps. We got to select breakfasts, dinners, and snacks from the ALE supply store. These were all meals that could be made by only adding hot water. We also received a "going to the bathroom" lecture for the low and high camps.

There we would be using the disposal toilet method, which we would use with the help of an empty bucket for our seating comfort. The "portable" toilets were personal of course and we would need to carry them with us, until our return to base camp so they could be "packaged" with the other bathroom "matters".

We also did "arts and crafts" and built a VINSON sign from snow. This sign is created once every season. Our lead guide Tre-C and I spearheaded the undertaking of this task for 2018. Some of my teammates also got some exercise filling the hole of the previous seasons' "freezer" tent. Every year when ALE staff opens the camp, the location of the tent needs to move back a few feet. The old hole then needs to be filled in again with snow, and because we were the first group of the season, and weather kept us just lazing around and enjoying great food, we needed to burn some calories!

December 1st, 2018, the weather became promising and our guides made the decision for us to move to low camp. We packed our gear into our backpacks and placed some supplies on the sleds. The suggested ratio was 70/30, backpacks to sleds.

The hiking time from base camp to low camp was about 5-6 hours. We took a break about every 60 to 90 minutes; standard mountaineering practice. Breaks were used to catch our breath, eat a couple of snacks, drink some water and pee.

Once we got to low camp, the area was more rudimentary in comparison to base camp, but more normal to climbing mountains. We had to set-up our own tents, but ALE maintains tents stored on-site, so we didn't carry them with us to low camp. Due to high winds, they cannot be left up when not in use, like in base camp. Our tents here were the standard three person tents, shared between two people. Emmanuel and I shared one.

The kitchen tent was also more basic and not heated as it was in base camp, but it had two separate seating areas with benches carved out of snow and a middle section for cooking. The double wall clam tent was pretty nice!

From here we could see the ridge of where the ropes started and go as high as 1200 m (close to 4000 feet) that we would have to climb to move to high camp. We could also see Vinson's Summit peak and the wind blowing snow at the top of the ropes and on the Summit. We needed to wait for a break in the weather to move to high camp.

Two other groups were also here, having moved from base camp to low camp with us.

The next day, we did a small hike to the start of the fixed ropes and practiced ascending the rope until about the third switch and then practiced descending.

I remember jumping over my first ever crevasse. Even though it was small, I really only had to do a small hop over, it took my breath away in fright. I did not know what awaited me in Everest.

December 2nd, 2018, weather was still bad up at high camp, however, because we were also a little restless from not doing much, except eating great food and sleep, some of us went on a hike to nearby peaks.

Steve and Seba went on their own. Tre-C and Lakpa took five of us for a view of the pyramid. Three of our colleagues had decided that they prefer to stay back at camp and "chill".

It was a 2 to 3-hour return hike but the view was amazing. We saw a pyramid literally standing out from the snow. The pyramid was the actual location of the old base camp. At the top of the small peak that we climbed to, we took a break, ate a snack and took pictures. Tre-C had some dress-up articles in her backpack, which gave us the opportunity to take funny pics! Purple was Emmanuel's color. He looked awesome with the purple wig.

On December 3rd, 2018 the winds still prevailed up top. We rested, read, slept.

On December 4th, our guides rally our team to move up to high camp, as they were confident with a predicted two day window break in the weather. We only packed our sleeping bags, water bottles, food, snacks, medication, and our clothing layers necessary into our backpacks. Our sleds also stayed behind. We took down our tents. We left any supplies and any equipment that we did not need up in high camp inside our duffle bags, and ALE stored them by the kitchen tent.

Another advantage of climbing with ALE in Vinson, is that the group does not have to carry up group gear, like fuel, tents, or even sleeping pads. ALE has all that at each camp. Each season ALE's guides and rangers, in anticipation of the climbing season, restock supplies for each team. Other companies must do "carries" and "cache" supplies, which means their climber teams take supplies to a camp one-day and return down to the previous camp. They then move up to the next camp the following day.

The climb up to high camp included a climb of about 1,200 meters, with an approximate 45 degree angle on the side of a mountain, aided by fixed ropes. We had to use our ascenders' and cows' tails to move on the fixed ropes and for safety. We took breaks, some just beside rocks but still roped in together.

I found the climb ok, with the exception of the last transfer point. I had looked up to see Seba, our guide, positioning his feet on a very narrow part of the terrain. My fear of heights rose immediately with my heart rate threatening to deafen me. I tried to concentrate, following his footsteps, completely aware I would have to climb down. I forced those thoughts out of my mind and concentrated on continuing the ascent. I would deal with descending another day.

When we reached high camp, both Wes and Nate, two of ALE's rangers that had gone up ahead of us to "open" camp, had our tents set-up and ready for us to go inside and rest, after we removed our crampons of course and made sure that our other "sharpies" were at a safe distance from our tents.

We were the Vinson 1 team, and therefore the first set of climbers of the season. This meant the pee hole still needed to be done, as did the placement of the "toilet" bucket.

We were able to admire the surroundings and the view from this height. Dinner was served inside our tents, after our guides' boiled water for our drinking pleasure and our dehydrated food preparation. I enjoyed my oatmeal. Emmanuel complained about his Spicy Pad Thai and repeated a few times to me how he hated dehydrated meals; this after he had lectured me previously that I needed to eat more than just oatmeal. But my oatmeal looked pretty good he admitted.

The dehydrated food I had in Rainer had made me feel awful and I know I did not want to feel this way in Vinson. Dehydrated food upsets my stomach. I have tried it several other times after Rainer and tasted various commercially available brands. I didn't and don't like any of them. And I was not going to risk an upset stomach in a continent made of white snow! Even energy bars cause me issues. That is why I had only chosen oatmeal for breakfast and dinners and for snacks I stuck with my Suzie's Good Fats Peanut Butter Chocolate Snack Bars.

Other teams arrived shortly after us and got busy setting up their own camp. One of the teams had just come up to drop a cache and then they went back down to low camp. This actually proved to be a dumb mistake on their part, as they became stuck in Vinson because of weather. But that's a completely different story that deals with egos and mountaineering.

After "dinner", Tre-C discussed with us our plan for the next day and suggested we go to sleep. We were hoping we would Summit the next day. We had only predicted two days of good weather, so we would not be spending the following day acclimatizing and resting in high camp, as sometimes happens. I honestly felt rested enough and was happy with this announcement. I just wanted to go up. Aside from seven blisters on both my feet, I was fine and looking forward to moving.

The next morning, we would have an early start – before 10:00 am. So, as usual, I pulled my hat around my ears and over my eyes to "shut the blinds" from the sun and went to sleep.

On Wednesday morning – Summit day – the sun was out! I had gotten used to it being daylight 24 hours a day, but somehow the sun shining over high camp was particularly special.

Getting ready to go to the summit was the same as with all other climbs. Our guides woke us up early, well, in Vinson it was at 8:30 am and bright daylight so there was no need for a headlamp! We got ready, had breakfast in our tent and started moving.

Tre-C had suggested we put hand warmers inside our mittens, accessible in our backpacks, ready to be used as it gets cold on the Summit Ridge. I did as she suggested. We had a different pair of gloves.

We continued our climb from high camp, roped in our teams of four, and we gained another 1000 m by the time we reached the summit.

Unlike Elbrus where we dropped our backpacks for the last summit push, here we kept our backpacks and I am happy we did, as it ensured I had all my flags.

Just before the summit, for about 15-20 minutes we had to walk on a thin ridge, snow iced and snow covered, with rocks, and a few boulders thrown into the path. This was daunting to me, but the excitement inside me was mounting.

Because each team member was roped together, the fellow climber in front of me kept pulling me forward, no doubt in his own anxiety. But that increased my anxiety. I was surprised that on the thin ridge, where I find I had to use self-talk to remind myself to, "Keep moving Ema! Don't look down." I didn't freak out. I kept thinking that the Summit of Vinson Massif was just in front of me. Just in front of me.

And then we were there! When we reach the summit, it was clear. No wind. It was beautiful!

There was a larger area, like a small plateau. It was wider than I ever imagined and we were allowed to unclip from each other and take our backpacks off.

I was elated. I felt like I was on top of the world. Wait a sec, I WAS on top of the world! Or some will argue the bottom of the World! It was Antarctica!

Lakpa Sherpa and his rope team were still there, as they were just ahead of us, and he graciously became my photographer for all my flags.

Sebastian mentioned to me that this was the first summit ever for him to have anyone wear such thin gloves, as he gestures to me just wearing my liner gloves. I didn't need my mittens or hand warmers that were inside my backpack today. Our parkas were also accessible in our backpacks, but there was no need for them at the top of the summit on this particular day. I couldn't believe I was at the summit of Vinson Massif.

Emmanuel searched for a small rock for me that I brought back for Ethan, my grandson. I had almost forgotten, but Emmanuel remembered for me.

Then it was time to leave and make our way back, so we could make room for other climbers that were attempting to summit as well.

It was a long way back to high camp and we didn't arrive until 8:30 pm. We were tired. I welcomed the comfort of my sleeping bag in a way I can't describe. We were planning to get an early start down the next day as the weather was threatening to turn.

So, the next morning, the plan was to descend from high camp, with a quick stop at low camp, then proceed all the way to base camp. It was going to be a long day.

The next day it was not the hiking on snow, or in the wind that had picked up exactly as our ALE guides had predicted, that fazed me or scared me, it was getting on and coming down the fixed lines.

My fear of heights got the best of me, for the first two to three ropes. I was scared as I saw a chocolate bar fall from our fellow climber David's hands or pocket. The chocolate bar, which we first thought was his phone, fell into the abyss as he was getting on the fixed ropes.

The first rope was so tight with tension that it was hard to clip in. Emmanuel was going backwards on this rope and had told me to go backwards too but our guide Sebastian told me to turn around and face forward. I listened to Sebastian of course, he was our guide, but turning around in an upright angle, in such a small space of snow only served to increase my anxiety. I know Emmanuel was just trying to get me not to see how high we were but my mind knew!

I had a mini panic attack on the second line, as I needed to transfer from one rope to another, and all I could see was my feet needing to be precise in their positioning, or I would fall. I knew I was tied in and our guide had the line secure on his prusik, but I also knew if I fell it would be a big deal for me mentally to get up again. I panicked. It was hard to breathe. I felt my airways suffocating me.

Emmanuel told me to focus and relax. Breathe. He told me that I could do it and that I was ok, I was not going to fall. It was kind of him to say so. He knew I needed help in that moment.

I relaxed after a few breaths and we continued down, slowly, line after line. I knew I needed to calm myself down and, thinking forward to other mountains, believe in myself more. I've got this. And Jesus has me!

Once back at base camp a celebratory dinner awaited us, with three bottles of champagne to celebrate our successful summit the day before. I had a glass, but somehow alcohol did not taste the same in the mountains. It was kind of anti-climactic.

We were hoping the next day we could fly to Union Glacier and get on the scheduled flight back to Punta Arenas, so we could fly home as planned on December 10th. But the weather did not cooperate and we waited. The next day was the same thing, more waiting.

But unlike in Carstensz Pyramid, I wasn't ill, and the food was amazing. The pure silence and beauty that surrounded us relaxed me and filled me with awe.

On December 9th we finally had a break in the weather and flew back to Union Glacier. As ALE clients we were on the first flight from base camp to Union Glacier.

We missed the Ilyushin, even though it had not flown into Union as scheduled, its delay was not enough for us to catch it. At that point, we were scheduled to leave Union back to Punta Arenas on the December 12th. It was disappointing.

When we arrived back at Union Glacier, we lined up for a shower! Ahhhhh... clean again. I was reminded of life's simple blessings. Here the water was melted snow, and we each of us had the equivalent of a large bucket of water only. Amazingly, it was more than enough.

Afterwards we got a behind the scenes tour of Union Glacier. Union Glacier is also the starting and end point of all kinds of people going on different types of adventures. For example, I met Richard Parks, who was the first person to do a grand slam, complete the 7 summits and ski the North and South Poles in less than 1 year. Is that even humanly possible I asked myself? Apparently so! He was trying to beat his solo record from the Hercules Inlet to the South Pole, a distance of 1140 km. He had been trying to do it in 25 days however, due to illness, his solo attempt ended prematurely, early in the New Year. There was also an Italian fellow hanging around, waiting for the perfect weather to go skydiving.

I spoke for a bit with Richard during the couple of days we were waiting, and in one of our conversations he commented: "Courage is how you act and face your fears and learn from it".

My fear of heights was still present. I needed to learn how to control it more. I was learning.

Not only was I meeting amazing people on these climbs, but I was also facing things and growing in ways that surprised and delighted me. I was becoming a climber!

Four down; three (well four) to go. After all, the 7 Summits are actually eight!

CHAPTER 10
ACONCAGUA

I remember when Emmanuel had summited Aconcagua in 2017 by himself, just before I started climbing. He summited while guiding his group, on his third attempt.

My goal was to summit my first time and deep down in my heart, I wanted to impress Emmanuel. After Antarctica, I was once again climbing alone, but in a group.

On the way to Argentina, I had some travel issues. The Air Canada flight I was on turned around three and a half hours into the flight and went all the way back to Toronto. At the time, we were already over the Bahamas. This made my getting to Penitentes, Argentina, to catch up with my group and guides, after more than a 24 hour delay, difficult. Added to this was my missed connection after the 10 hour flight.

The next connecting flight would delay me yet another day. It was a stressful and frustrating start.

On February 5th, 2019 I was finally able to get to Argentina, after driving from Santiago, Chile and crossing the border by car. I felt somewhat flustered, as I had missed gear check scheduled the day before in Mendonza, and of course, I had missed valuable information on the expected climb, schedules, and more.

I was again climbing with Alpine Ascents, and Vern and Carole were my main guides. My room at the Ayelen Hotel in Penitentes was dismal, but maybe it was intentional to get us used to the tent and dirt in Aconcagua. It worked!

The green carpet in the room was worn including under the radiator where it was down to its last fibres. The bed was only a mattress against the wall on a cheap metal frame. Thin sheets. It was one of the worst hotels I had ever stayed in.

Penitentes is an old ski resort town, that is only now open during the short season that the Aconcagua National Park is open. It welcomes climbers or the occasional person passing through that may need a room.

Thankfully, I didn't stay there long. The day after my arrival, on Wednesday, February 6th, we made our way to the entrance of the Aconcagua National Park, to climb the normal route of the mountain. We stopped at the park ranger's office where our guides picked up our park permits. These cost $610.00 USD each! Whoa! We were then required to show our passports as identification before gaining entrance to the park.

The trek from the beginning of the trail to the Confluência Camp took about 3 hours. Our group's gear was being carried by mules, which on this particular day was very slow. I know. I know. Mules are supposed to be slow, but those ones were sedated slow. By the time they arrived at camp with our duffle bags it was around 9 pm!

While we waited, we had dinner. Some of us went for a short walk to the top of the hill to see the whole camp from "above". Our guides Vern and Carole taught us how to build a tent "Aconcagua" style so that our tents would have the best chance to resist the high winds and not blow away. This training would come in very handy! The Confluência Camp sits at 3,421 metres.

The camp had a medical office, staffed with a doctor employed by the park and whom we all had to go see the following day on Thursday, February 7th, to get the "green light" to move up the mountain to base camp on Friday, February 8th. This would be one of two visits with the park's doctor. The park authorities wanted to ensure climbers were not experiencing altitude related illness, which would cutdown on emergency rescues.

Our tents for this expedition were three person tents, but really only fit two people, and in very close quarters. My tentmate was Jenny, a young lady from Chicago in her mid 20's.

On Thursday February 7th, we went for a seven hour acclimatization hike towards Camp Francia, for a view of the south face of the mountain. The colours of all the rock faces on our way there were spectacular!

First it was hot, and then it got very windy and much colder as we reached about 14,000 feet, or about 4,000 metres.

Friday, February 8th, we made our way to Plaza de Las Mulas base camp for the normal route. It took us "eight hours plus one", as Vern said. For a long period of time, we hiked on flat terrain and then slowly gained altitude. The mules carried our group gear. Slowly.

What can I say about Plaza de Las Mulas? It's a tent city on a mountain plateau. We had to select our campsite and build our tent but that's ALL that was interesting.

Alpine Ascents local contractors were Aconcagua Mountain Guides, a subsidiary of Alpine Ascents. Inca, another outfitter at the camp, was clearly the prominent provider there. Their tents and facilities were at the entrance of the camp. I couldn't help but notice they were shinier and seemed new. I guess I was still spoiled from Antarctica and Vinson.

ACONCAGUA

Our campsite was on the opposite end of base camp, and it had its own benefits. It was closer to the trail to go up the mountain. That was the goal after all, to go up the mountain. Plus, it was quieter.

It was a long day. I personally wasn't able to get cell service though many people seem to. I was however able to buy Wi-Fi for the days we were there, so I was able to talk to my husband Steve, my daughters Nicole and Patricia and of course, my grandchildren Ethan and Julia. I always felt so alone on these climbs. Aconcagua proved to be no different.

On February 9th, we tried our crampons on, and practiced wearing them on the dirty snow. Afterwards, we went for a short 90 minute hike, over lots of rock, to ice sticking out of the mountain like icicles. These were called penitents. They were pretty cool. I never realized so much dirt could be on top of an actual glacier! It was the primary reason it was so dusty and a little disgusting there.

This outing was followed by a group meeting, to discuss the game plan for the next few days. Acclimatization is an important part of climbing, especially at this height, to have the best chance of success, so we decided to do a carry up to Camp Canada the following day. We would do the same the next day as well.

As mentioned in an earlier chapter, the "carry up" is done to carry a small amount of supplies to a higher camp and leave them there to be used once we move up to that camp. This exercise serves to acclimatize and also to lessen the weight of carrying the supplies needed, in our backpacks.

Porters were now available on the mountain and I took advantage of them. Seba in Vinson had suggested it. As a result, I did not do a "carry" of group gear or supplies. I was able to simply enjoy the acclimatization climb carrying only my daypack. The porters would carry my portion of the group gear and my personal supplies on "move" day. The plan was to do the same the next day and then move up the following day. The theory was again to climb high, sleep low.

On the second carry day, the winds were extremely high and we got hit with a snowstorm. The snow was basically small round ice pellets, not beautiful snowflakes. This was jarring and difficult.

We were offered a free shower because the mules had been late when we came into Confluencia a few days back at the previous camp. We all took advantage of it here at base camp, though the word "shower" was used loosely. The water was cold! And only served to rinse the dust off. Unfortunately, no one shared that you could simply move the lever a very short space to get warm water! Would have been nice to have that information before my shower.

February 12th was a rest day. We did nothing. We just ate and stayed in our tents actually. Pretty boring. One of the other female teammates went for a swim in a lake nearby, apparently skinny dipping. I passed.

On February 13th, we moved up to Camp Canada. It sits at 4947 metres, on a hill. If you take a wrong step, you might just fall off, but the view was amazing. "Ahhhhhh" had two meanings!

The porter assigned to me moved everything, I just kept my emergency gear in my backpack, a bottle of water and my personal documents like passport, insurance and money. It was great.

At Camp Canada, the rest of the group had all opted to use the services of the porters to set-up our tents. It was so much easier to reach camp and have a place to get comfortable in, sheltered from the cold and wind.

My tentmate and I kept getting a tent that had something wrong with it. Ugh. The tents were North Face and spacious, but they were so beat up and just didn't hold up. This time we were stuck with a vestibule zipper that was broken, so we literally had to crawl in and out of our tent.

On February 14th, we did a carry to what would be our second camp, Nido de Condores. It was a 3 hour hike up. It was a huge camp, amazing 360 degree views! There were mountainous peaks and vast sky as far as the eye could see. Spectacular! There was also a rangers' station and a helipad.

Going back down to Camp Canada took only an hour that day.

One of our teammates Sequoia had reported a headache and Diego, one of our guides raced down the mountain with her to Camp Canada. The rest of us followed. My feet were sweating with the socks I had chosen and I got two blisters. However not much to complain about in the grand scheme.

When we got back to Camp Canada, there was hardly walking space between tents. There were tents everywhere around us. Seems everyone at base camp was moving up. There were climbers galore.

Sequoia however was still not feeling well. She was still reporting headaches and Carole accompanied her down to base camp to see the doctor who diagnosed her with altitude sickness. She was not allowed to continue climbing.

The plan for the rest of the group was to continue our climb. On February 15th, the day after Valentine's Day, we moved to Nido de Condores, which stands at 5560 metres. From this vantage point it seemed like we were higher than all the mountains around us.

While at camp, a group came down with a person on a stretcher. I did not take any pictures; it felt in bad taste to do so, even though many other climbers were. The person was clearly in distress and very sick.

Moments later the yellow rescue helicopter hovered over us, landed and took the individual away. He looked gravely ill. Later we learned that the person had fallen ill the day before at 7:00 pm, just below summit, and was only then being rescued at about 3:00 pm. He had to be brought up by foot. My heart went out to him.

During our first night at this camp, Nido de Condores, I woke up suffocating. Short of breathe. I was taking Diamox but I couldn't breathe. I had a really hard time sleeping for the first time on a mountain. We were very high at 5522 meters, about 18,117 ft, in altitude and it was cold. When I woke around 1:45 am, I could not breathe. I was gasping for air. I peed in my pee bottle and drank a hot drink from my Thermos to try and sort myself out. I laid down again and I still could not breathe. My nose was stuffy and I could not catch my breath. I began pressure breathing, and it helped, but I still could not get enough air. Then I put on my ColdAvenger mask and I took another quarter of my Diamox pill. After a little bit, I was finally able to feel some relief. It was the scariest experience I had had thus far. I did not understand what was going on. I really thought I might suffocate.

Later in the morning I was surprised to receive a text message from Emmanuel, that simply read: "How did you sleep?". Tears filled my eyes as I responded. "Ok, but I woke up feeling like I couldn't breathe. I mean really couldn't breathe. I took more Diamox."

Emmanuel reassured me when he said, "It's normal. You are up high. It's sleep apnea. Try sleeping more upright; put all your clothes under your sleeping pad to sleep more upright."

"Ok." I typed back. But I felt emotional and scared remembering I had been gasping for air the night before. I felt so alone.

"It's the altitude. You are doing great! And you will be ok," he responded. He was a man of few words but still surprised me that he knew how I may be feeling. I guess having been there himself several times helped. He was tracking my climbing of course and had known from experience what I may have been feeling. I was so grateful for his text and advice, and for him caring.

When I had shared my ordeal with Steve, he was dismissive. I felt so lonely. I held onto Emmanuel's message for the next couple of days, so I could feel cared for and that I mattered.

On February 16th we woke up cold, and I mean frigid cold. It would remain that way until the sun hit the mountain and warmed the tent. I regretted not bringing my other sleeping bag with me. The plan for today had been to do a group carry to the 3rd and final camp, Camp Colera. It was high. We would reach an altitude of 19,580 feet, about 5,970m and we were planning to move there tomorrow.

I got really cold in the early hours of the morning so I put my red Canada Goose jacket on. I also used the ColdAvenger mask over my face to be able to breathe more easily. The air is so dry there, it felt like a desert, but a cold desert. Somehow it felt colder than Antarctica. We made the move to Camp Colera, or Camp 3, as planned the next day.

It had been a long way up. One of our teammates had diarrhea and was really slow and tired. Camp Colera was given the name by the guides because people vomit and poop so much there. An ugly fact, but true.

This camp was on an enclave of a huge rock, with a view of the Aconcagua Summit. Usually, people stay here no more than a couple of nights, but it seemed we would spend three in total. We planned to have a rest day and then attempt the Summit on Tuesday, February 19th.

I decided to lay in my parka inside my sleeping bag. What a huge difference in warmth that made!

Early in the morning of our rest day February 18th, we heard another group get up for their summit bid. They were a little noisy. A couple of hours later, I heard a guide bring back one of their female clients who had been turned around. I could only imagine her disappointment.

On February 19th, we started our summit bid at 6:00 am. It was freezing but we were ready. Lynn, one of our teammates who was 70 years old (a perfect example that age is only relative to how you feel), was ready too and we started our summit bid. Then all I heard was something about sunglasses and then he was no longer going up with us. I was confused but just kept moving.

We go up slowly, and it took us about nine and a half hours to reach the Summit. The last thirty minutes were hard. With every step I took it seemed harder to breathe.

I was puffing my cheeks out (like a chipmunk, like Vern had taught us) and exhaling. I was also straightening my body in combination with my rest step, to allow more air to fill my lungs. But I still struggled.

Vern climbs in front of me and says: "You can do this Ema. We are almost there."

I simply reply, "These rocks are hard; there are so many rocks."

Vern replies in a very Vern like tone of voice: "No fucking shit, you are climbing a mountain!" It made me laugh.

I had read that to reach the summit, we had to go through the "La Canaleta" which is a scramble up some rocks. I think that would be true if we could truly scramble up rock, but since there was enough snow to wear crampons on certain sections, I am not sure that qualified as a scramble.

At the base of the so-called "La Canaleta", there was a rocky, concave-base wall somewhat in the shape of a cave, "La Cueva". Here we were at 6650 meters, or 21,817 feet.

We summited on February 19th, at 3:40 pm local time.

It was windy up at the summit, and in my first couple of pictures, my flag was upside down. Then I corrected it, but the wind made it hard. Vern offered to hold the flag on one of the corners. It worked – kinda.

Then it was time to come down, just like that. All that effort and strain and it's over in a few minutes. But I did it.

I did it.

It was a long way down. It took us close to five hours. I was so tired, that I kept slipping and falling on my behind. There was a ridge right after Independencia Refuge that's considered the world's tallest refuge. One must make it across the ridge to make it to the La Canaleta section before the summit, and then back on the return.

The wind is generally very strong in this area since it's exposed. A slip here could mean you fall thousands of meters down the face of the mountain. It is where many expeditions turn around on the way to the summit when the weather is bad. We were told this earlier when Carole had shown us how we should climb and brace ourselves at this point on summit day. Luckily, we had great weather. Hardly any wind in this section on that day. Unusual. I knew Jesus had me. I had begged for hours asking Jesus for no wind.

About an hour left in our descent I started seeing what I thought was a fly, or a flying spider, on the right hand side of my eye. Because I was wearing my goggles, I thought there were bugs outside, since the sun was also starting to set. But the site of this 'bug' was actually something I was only seeing on my right eye. I continued to see the 'bug' until the day after we left the mountain. According to my daughter Nicole, a Nurse Practitioner, they were "floaters" that I was seeing. I am fortunate that they have since disappeared.

The following day we made our descent from Camp 3 all the way to base camp. It was a long day. When we reached base camp we were treated to hamburgers. I had a veggie burger. The team shared a bottle of champagne, courtesy of Alpine Ascents, and our generous guides Vern, Carole and Diego. It was a much needed celebration!

A couple of our teammates, including our Canuck friend, had a few too many beers. I no longer had an interest in drinking at high altitude and it amazed me how some could. But that's me and everyone is different.

February 21st, we take the long trek from base camp to the park exit. This in itself was a wonderful experience because how often can one say they trekked on a riverbed?

After we exited the park, we picked our stuff up from storage, and continued by bus back to Mendoza. That evening I took my "first" shower in three weeks. I had never been so dirty in my life!

Kudos to the Hyatt staff that checked me in and never showed any expression regarding how dirty my face was. It shocked me when I looked at myself in the bathroom mirror. I had not looked at my face in the mirror while on the mountain so it was a bit of a shock!

Back to hygiene. Back to cleanliness. I was going home! I had completed Aconcagua on my first attempt.

Only two (well 3) more to go... Seven (8) Summits for Mental Health.

CHAPTER 11
DENALI

On June 28, 2019, I climbed the tallest mountain in North America, and became the first Portuguese woman to do so. The first Portuguese Canadian woman to do so.

I stood on the Summit for about 20 minutes, and even though it might not seem much, it was a lot.

The thought of Denali used to scare me. Maybe it was that Denali prep-course I had taken back in July 2017 that scared me. The memories of three broken ribs five weeks prior and carrying an 80L backpack stuffed with more than sixty pounds, up Mount Rainier had scared me. The memories of how I felt with the all-women team climbing was still on my mind and gave me doubts. Added to the mix was my memory of Antarctica, on Vinson Massif, descending the fixed line, where I had frozen in fear of falling during the first couple of anchors. I recalled my friend Emmanuel saying if I was afraid there, I would never make it to Denali. Denali scared me.

Denali is the tallest mountain, aside from Everest, however from its base, it actually has a higher altitude gain then climbing Everest itself, whose base camp stands already at approximately 17,598 feet, or 5,364m.

Denali, or Mount McKinley, in Alaska is also known to have very bad weather.

Our permit to climb, meaning to be in the National Park was for twenty two days, which allowed fifteen days inside the park to climb with perfect conditions and seven extra days for back-up.

Success rate of reaching the Summit is usually 50%, however in 2019 year it increased to approximately 61%.

I climbed, summited, and was out of the state park within twelve days of entering it.

No, it was not easy. But no, it was not the two-headed monster I envisioned and had read about in other climber's accounts, or even what I had watched in YouTube videos.

There were no toes lost to frostbite, nor did any of us fall into a crevasse where we hung for hours.

Climbing Denali though was the hardest, most physical and mentally challenge thing I had done in my life. It took a lot of self-perseverance, prayers and begging Jesus for help, but also a firm determination that I wanted to complete this ascent and not return to try again.

My journey started in Anchorage Alaska. I climbed Denali with Mountain Trip. It was a private expedition.

I arrived in Anchorage in the evening and checked into the hotel. I arrived with a very heavy heart. My mother-in-law Bonnie, had been diagnosed as "failure to thrive" and moved to a hospice room for the family to say goodbye. I was not there. I felt I should be, that I needed to be, but as I had been about to board my flight to Anchorage from my layover in the US, I had asked Steve on the phone if I should turn around and come back home.

"Don't be an idiot!" was his response. I never knew if it was support for me to continue or if he didn't want me around to support him.

Bonnie passed away Monday June 17th, my day two of this trip.

I felt so conflicted. Guilty. I had been married for more than twenty years and yet, this brought about the stark realization that I was not needed or wanted in my marriage. I know I was personally stronger at this point but I still loved Steve, even after all his betrayal and lies. I would have gone home for the funeral in a heartbeat, had he asked. He did not.

The following morning, I met my three guides; Kaylee, Jason and Ryan, and we did my gear check. I was feeling a little sick as I had eaten some vegetarian tacos at the hotel's restaurant the afternoon before and they did not agree with me. In the middle of the night, I managed to throw up and then started to hydrate myself. I couldn't be sick for my first day! This was Denali and I felt enough pressure as it was.

On Tuesday, June 18, 2019, we flew to base camp. To get there we drove approximately two or three hours from Anchorage to Talkheeta before taking an Air Taxi for a twenty minute short flight over amazing scenery.

Once we touched down in base camp, we took all our gear off the runway and set up our first "camp".

Kaylee gave me my first lesson, with Jason giving his stamp of approval and further suggestions, on how to set-up our tent in our first "camp".

As we enjoyed dinner, sitting on the snow, I marveled how much snow there was. I took a few deep breaths and silently pray to God for Him to guide me and asked Him to have my back, because I was scared of what lay ahead. Every so often you heard avalanches in the distance. I had butterflies in my stomach, as the stories and videos I'd watched on YouTube about climbing Denali weighed heavy in my mind.

I also felt a lot of anxiety. I wanted, needed, to summit to become the first Portuguese Canadian woman to summit Denali. I reminded myself; this was Denali. I was on the "big league" mountain. I never imagined in my wildest dreams I would be there. But I was. I was there.

After our tents were made, we took some supplies out to sleep, since we were going to move during the night when the snow was colder and more compact. It was mushy at that moment.

Then it started snowing.

After a few hours, it was a new day. We woke up early, two in the morning, and got ready to start hiking. Kaylee was like a tornado! Within seconds, she had her sleeping bag in its pack and she was ready to head out. All the while I was trying to stuff my mammoth sleeping bag from Western Mountaineering in its compression bag. I stepped out and she had her harness on.

She was supposed to be a guide in training, climbing as my third private guide to make my climb easier, but I was surprised and very impressed. That was fast!

I was thrown off a little by how fast things were moving. I felt agitated. I needed the bathroom and there was someone in the green bucket. I waited.

Let me explain the green bucket. You get them in Talkeetna from the park rangers, and this is your bathroom while on the mountain for your poop. You must bring the bucket back, with all its contents once you are off the mountain. You need to try not to pee in the bucket because urine will freeze, which becomes ice. If it does, you have to carrying heavy "ice blocks" up and down the mountain.

When we finally got going, pulling the sled was not that challenging. Stepping over a crack (crevasse) that would be wider when we return however, was a little unsettling.

At the mere sight of one, my heart would start beating so fast, anxiously, and I sometimes thought it would stop and I would die. I would later experience much worse in Everest, but I was in Denali now.

We made it to Camp 1 in six hours and thirty minutes. Jason our lead guide said it was good time. I was glad. It was 8:30 am local time.

After tents were up, there was nothing else to do but lay down and try to sleep or just rest. These forced rests are the not so easy part of climbing. I texted Steve and the kids and felt better.

Steve was making funeral arrangements and again a wave of guilt washed over me. Our conversations were unemotional. Part of me wished I was there to help, but I knew I would not be able to in terms of arrangements. Seemed they had it covered, even though Steve said everyone seemed angry and upset at the moment. I knew that was normal in these difficult circumstances.

Suddenly, the sun came out and we got a great view of Denali. I marveled at how impressive and majestic the mountain was. It was giant! Denali was a gorgeous creation of God.

Then a cloud went over the sun and the temperature dropped considerably. This was the same on every mountain. You could easily go from a wonderful warm temperature to a cold one in a matter of minutes, sometimes seconds it seemed.

As we climbed, there was nothing much to do other than count numbers in your head and think. Here life seemed surreal, easy. But in the back of my mind was a mild, gnawing tension, missing my family and my life at home.

The silence and the loneliness of climbing mountains brought up many feelings. I missed my family and Steve. It also brought up the realization that I needed to change my life if I was ever to breathe again, feel human again.

Climbing any mountain puts you in the realm of being uncomfortable; hot, cold, lonely, tired, and sometimes hungry. It pushes your physical capacity to the limit. You enter survival mode. But I found with each step it also made me stronger. Emotionally and slowly physically.

I was there to climb the highest mountain in the northern hemisphere. I needed to concentrate. The plan was to move to Camp 2 the following day, leaving at the same time around 2 am.

However, we did not move to Camp 2. We woke up as planned at 2 am, and Kaylee told us she had been feeling sick all night and had thrown up a couple of times. I hadn't heard her, even though we shared a tent.

I instinctively knew it was from our dinner the night before. It was the pre-made salad we had bought at our last supply stop before arriving in Talkeetna. It had mayonnaise. I had passed on my own.

Kaylee said we would have to go slowly, which sounded good to me. When she told her colleagues, the decision was made to stay put and let her sleep until she felt better. Reaching a higher camp not feeling well would drain her and limit her ability to acclimatize and be strong enough to summit. If that was the case, we would then need to turn around.

I hated just waiting around and doing nothing, but there was nothing we could do. I had trust in Jesus, and his reasons.

I advised the kids and Steve, even though he had his hands full, what was happening. It was his mom's viewing and I knew it would be taking a toll on him. The funeral had been the next day. A few months later he would tell me how unemotional he had been during all of this and tried to convince me he had Alexithymia (a problem feeling emotions), during one of our arguments.

I forced myself to concentrate on the mountain. When the sun was out, it was hot. Sun and snow was like sun and sand. I learned how to use the solar panel and understand that since it had a built in battery, it could not take a lot of heat, I had to be careful with it.

Then I saw a familiar face, Sebastian (Seba) my guide from Antarctica. He and his client, Aparna, a lady from India that was trying to climb Denali for the third time, arrived in camp. Aparna had done all the mountains, including Everest and she did the North side. I was inspired.

This was my official day five. The climbing portion of the day seemed extremely long. I don't know why. It was just a long day. It started with getting up at 1:00 am, actually I had been up a little earlier. Days and nights stretched and shortened. It was difficult.

We packed everything. Backpacks and sleds were loaded about two hours later, and we started climbing towards Camp 2.

Some teams take caches to about 11,000 feet and then go back to Camp 1, then the following day go up to Camp 2 with a lesser load. We climbed with our complete load and honestly, I am glad because after climbing the steep hill between Camp 1 and 2, once was enough.

Camp 2 in Denali was set in a small plateau. We were not allowed to walk very far, because there was a huge crevasse (crack as they call it). It was colder here, even with the sun shining full blast. But it was very pretty! One is surrounded by smaller peaks with Denali imposing itself in one corner. It was a breathtaking sight.

The white of the snow and blue skies made it extra magical.

The following day Ryan, our assistant guide and Kaylee went up to Camp 14, which is how everyone refers to it, but really it's Camp 3. They took a cache, which should be called stash instead. It holds some of our supplies and keeps them "stashed" so that we don't have to carry them all at once. I thought I was supposed to go, but then only Kaylee and Ryan went. I stayed behind to go over some skills with Jason my lead guide.

After breakfast, I put my crampons and harness on, got my ice axe, and we went through a couple of basics including foot work on crampons, proper ice arrest, how to hold the ice axe, and then we were done. The repetition of basic but necessary skills calms me. So many people here were attempting Denali for the second and third time. I really hoped I could do this! I have been silently praying to Jesus, but I needed to pray out loud and beg him for his hand holding and good weather!

On June 25th, the day of the expedition, we were at the 14,000 ft. camp. The weather was ok, but definitely colder. We had moved up here on Sunday. It was here that my inReach froze. I had a panic attack because I could no longer communicate with the kids and Steve. I felt lost, like that feeling you get when you can't find your cell phone.

It was hard. It was a tough push up Motorcycle Hill, then Squirrel Hill and on Windy Corner, we had to put our helmets on. My helmet tends to sit on me sideways but that time it didn't. Thank you Lord!

If you're asking yourself what do all these hill names mean or who gave the names, I don't have the answer. I asked a few people and no one really seemed to know. It's not like there were motorcycles or squirrels up there!

Anyway, on Windy Corner (this name I can understand), Jason said we could not stop at all, as it was always windy. There was a small ledge on the snow to walk on, but I barely thought about it. There was no wind. None. And that was unusual. Why? Well, my theory was of course that Jesus was next to me holding my hand; guiding me and taking care of the weather. Just like he had done in Aconcagua, at the start of the ridge known as Portezuelo del Viento, towards the Canelata. Jesus Rocks!

Like Carole in Aconcagua, Jason also commented what great weather we were having at that very moment.

When we finally got to Camp 3, or should I say, Camp 14. It was cloudy and the clouds kept rolling by, underneath us. To be high in the sky with clouds rolling past you is an indescribable experience. It's like you are on a Philadelphia cream cheese commercial, the one with the Angel sitting on top of the clouds.

To my great surprise I saw the Thai lady here that I saw in Vinson. She was climbing with another Mountain Trip team. It was only her and a German male climber. It definitely is a small world. I knew she told me her name this time, as we spoke, but I regrettably can't remember it. In Vinson, she had been climbing with Adventure Consultants and an older Thai gentleman that I learned in Denali was not her father, just another climber.

I was happy I did a private trip so we could climb based on how I was feeling and according to my pace. I was happy to have shared a tent with Kaylee. The group that started when we did, Kristen's group, had males and females sharing tents, which at first made me uncomfortable. I didn't think I would feel okay sharing a tent with a stranger of the opposite sex, but looking back now, it probably had more to do with my own confidence and self-esteem, not to mention Steve being in my head projecting some of these feelings on me. Sharing a tent in the mountains is for safety only, regardless of tent mate gender. Plus it has the added bonus of having someone you can talk to.

The battery from the inReach died completely at one point, but I had been able to restart it and charge it. I had begged Jesus during my hike for a couple of hours, so much so I think I got on his nerves and he just gave in.

The following day we went to get the cache back down after windy corner and came back to camp. Then we had a rest day. It was nice being able to change clothes and spend the morning relaxing. I learned that relaxing is part of acclimatization. It's an important mountaineering life lesson.

On June 26, our tenth day of the expedition, we climb from our camp at 14,000 feet up to 17,000 feet. High camp. We had made the decision to move up and not remain the usual number of days at Camp 14, because we were all feeling good, acclimatized and Jason had seen a bit of a weather was due in a couple of days. So, we went for it.

I can't lie... it was hard. The fixed lines were surprisingly the easiest to do, but there were high stretches and really thin walking sections along the ridges.

Luckily I felt Jesus had me through this climb. My lead guide Jason had a rope closer to me and brought it in closer on more exposed sections to help me out. Bless him. It made all the difference in the world with my anxiety. Did I already tell you I am afraid of heights?

To give you an idea of what it feels like, it's something like this: my heart races really fast, so fast it's like I hear the blood going in and out of my heart. I feel my heart itself against my chest. I have difficulty breathing and my thoughts become negative and my body starts to become paralyzed.

I knew I had to go back down though, a fact that did not escaped me. Just like in Vinson. But I just kept moving and to be honest, once we reach the camp at 17,000 feet, or Camp 4, my attention shifted. We had arrived at a scene from a movie in a wild snowy desert. It was unreal. There were ice walls everywhere and very few tents.

It was also cold (colder) up there. I was shivering so much, that Jason actually gave me his parka and instructed me to put it on, while a couple tents were set up. I helped as much as I could, but I was freezing. I guess the anxiety of the last hundred or so feet of intense heights and small ridges had sent my body into shock and now it had no energy to warm itself up. I was probably also dehydrated. Anxiety and drinking water don't always go together.

There was no kitchen tent there. Ryan and Jason bring myself and Kaylee hot water in thermoses to make our food; dehydrated meals, noodles and oatmeal.

I was peeing in my pee bottle and going out to empty it or use the big green bucket, whatever nature called for. We were planning a summit attempt the next morning. Jason was looking very closing at the tight weather window.

The next morning, we got ready and were on our way at about 8:30 am. The sky was blue with not a cloud in sight. I was wearing my puffy pants, but had my parka in my backpack, along with snacks, my thermos of hot water, my inReach, my cell phone in the pocket of my lightweight puffy jacket, and of course mittens, goggles, and sunscreen to re-apply constantly.

We set out towards the Autobahn and no, not the German highway, it's a steep climb on the side of a mountain, which was slow going. I had asked Jason why it was called the Autobahn, and with a smile on his face he replied, "because if you slip and fall, you are going to come down REALLY fast". It was so slow it took us about two hours, and my lead guide, Jason was not too happy about it. "Ema, how are you doing?"

"Ok." I replied, half out of breath.

"Really? Every time I look back, it seems the rope is pushing. Two hours is not bad time, actually it's average for a normal group, but we should go faster with our small group." Jason states. I say nothing.

We stopped a couple of times during the climb for Ryan, my other guide who had called "stop". I had welcomed the break, but Ryan was feeling sick and nauseous. Turns out the dehydrated dinner from the previous night did not agree with him. I saw Jason hand him an anti-nausea pill.

I found this section hard. The ingrained steps on the snow, set from the hundreds of climbers throughout the season, were big "risers" in certain sections for my short legs. When I took a higher, longer step, I felt out of breath. I felt we were moving fast, which did not allow me to breathe properly during my rest steps. The harder I breathed, the harder it became to climb and thus I became slower.

"Well, let's continue and re-evaluate at the top of Zebra Rocks, and we can go from there. We will evaluate at every point" Jason says.

I said nothing and just move. I self-talked myself to pick up my pace, as I did not want to come back here. The huge expense was one thing, but I knew mentally I could not repeat this challenge. I concentrated on my deep breathing and kept focused. I begged Jesus to stay with me and push me up, with each step.

When we reach Zebra Rocks, Jason announced, "Great push guys. We made great time. Ema, great work. We are back on track."

I respond, "ok."

I knew I was the client and I could have pushed back if I wanted to, but I didn't. I hired them to help me and guide me. I was more determined than ever to reach the summit.

We continued to the next stage, then the next, until we were at the Summit Ridge. It was tall, well obviously – but it was also thin and exposed. My heart raced so fast.

Jason reassured me that Ryan had my rope closer to him and if I felt scared or needed them to go slower, to just let Ryan know. Jason was leading our rope team, followed by Kaylee, then Ryan and then myself. I was really scared.

Like reading my mind, Jason reassured me, "being last on the rope is the best place, because if you slip, you have three bodies to hold you and get you back up. Not that you are going to fall!"

I only mumbled, "ok."

I am not going to sugar coat it; I was anxious. Ryan was a wonderful guide and he constantly reassured me that I was ok and that I was not going to fall. The closer we got to the summit, the more I believed him.

I took several deep breaths. I felt as if I was having an out of body experience.

As we were "walking" on the summit ridge, a couple of other groups were coming down. Meaning coming in the opposite direction we were going. One was a large group from Alpine Ascents and the other was an RMI group. We stopped and let them pass on the left hand side. Ryan tried to talk to me about trivial things to distract me as the other climbers passed us. There was not a lot of room, and we passed very close to each other.

The RMI group had a female guide among them and she looked at me as she passed, with seeming annoyance and superiority. For a brief moment I was again in Rainer, feeling small but I shook my head and said to myself, "I don't care. I am a few feet away from the Summit of Denali and she is inconsequential."

I had heard her a couple of times at lower camps screaming at members of her team and had thought how grateful I was not to be part of that group.

When we reach the summit, the area itself was larger than I anticipated. I took my cell phone out of my pocket to tell the world that I was at the summit. I was so excited and wanted it documented. My inReach message was sent with a GPS recorded location. I had become the first Portuguese woman to summit Denali. I was also the first Portuguese Canadian woman to have done so too.

We had time to take group pictures, individual pictures and pictures with all six of my flags. We attempted to call from the satellite phone three times, but the call kept dropping. I recorded a message to my family, that Mountain Trip would send to them. Jason called his fiancé.

Kaylee did a short run and jumped over the summit marker. It was fun at the summit! We had the whole summit space to ourselves. Jesus is so wonderful and caring. He had me. He brought me to the top of Denali. I know it helped that all four of us were believers and that back home, we all had people praying for us. Not a coincidence in my humble opinion.

There was no wind. It was sunny and so clear that I could see all the smaller mountains below us. I was elated. About twenty minutes later it was time to descend, so we started to make our way back down.

Jason explained that I was going to be in front, with the three of them behind me. He again reminded me of his rational and assurance that if I were to fall, I would have three guides holding me and I would not go anywhere. I understood his reasoning and began to descend.

Ryan was directly behind me, talking to me, "Slowly Ema. Take your time. You got this!" I walked slowly, but somehow confident. I stopped when Ryan told me, so he could secure his share of the rope to the fixed anchors. Then as he shouts back, "Climbing", we continued. We did this pattern many times.

Before I knew it, we were out of the ridge and were making our way down. Amazingly, we were going at a pretty good pace. So good in fact, that even with our generous standard breaks, we reached high camp at about 7:00 pm. This signified we took about 10.5 hours to summit and back.

I overheard the delight in Jason's voice, "10.5 hours puts us on the top 30% of top ascents. This is nuts!"

Kaylee giggled, but in a humble voice, said, "Well yeah, but these are abnormal conditions. Usually, the weather isn't this great!"

I thought to myself, "Yeah, so?" We did it, regardless of the weather.

The next morning, we started our descent back to base camp. We left early morning to get to 14,000 feet before it was too hot. We took a long rest at 14,000 feet, until the temperature cooled down, making it easier to walk on the snow.

At Camp 2 or 11,000 feet, we put our snowshoes back on replacing our crampons. The descent from here on was not easy. It was about 11:00 pm or just passed it. I should mention that during this time of year, it really never gets dark in Denali as well.

Even at this late hour, the snow in some areas was still mushy. I tripped several times. Jason was leading; I was in second position, with Kaylee behind me and Ryan in the back. He has the hardest job, trying to keep all our slides inline. I kept stumbling, and took a few falls, several times smacking my face directly on the snow. I fell a lot, especially when Jason's sled pulled me forward. With each stumble I would shout, "Stop". And everyone did. Each time as gracefully as possible, I got up and we all continued.

Ski Hill was especially hard, as the snow was really slippery. During one of our brief breaks, I ask what time it was. When Jason said, "It's 1:30 am" I said to Kaylee, "It's your birthday already – Happy Birthday!" The three of us made an attempt to sing Happy Birthday to Kaylee. The sun was rising again behind us, even though it had only set a couple of hours before.

When we finally reached Camp 1 there were several tents set-up, and another set of Mountain Trip guides were escorting a group of several Russian climbers.

Jason said, "We are going to take a longer break here, once they retrieved the cache that we left on the way up."

Ryan asked "Why?" and Jason replied, "Let's take our time. We are an hour ahead of schedule."

I was silently happy we were moving fast and think that falling so many times was not so embarrassing. I actually took it as symbolism of why I was climbing. You can fall, but you just need to get back up on your feet and keep moving. Like with mental health, we may fall but we get back up and keep going.

And so, we did. The walk out from Camp 1 towards base camp seemed endless.

I tried to recall my memory of walking up twelve days earlier but could not remember. I knew I made it, but with all the snow, I don't remember the route.

I was careful to keep following Jason's footsteps, as we walked around crevasses. I pulled my trekking poles up, careful not to stab the snow where Jason had just walked over a crevasse wall and moved as quickly as I could passed it, until the next one.

I kept thinking of Richard Parks, when he was doing his 737 Challenge, and had been on Denali in 2011, about the same time of the year, when he punched through a crevasse and fell really deep. He had to use his ice axe on the lip of the crevasse to get himself out. So, stabbing the snow now was out of the question.

We were back at base camp at about 5:30 am on June 30, hoping to get on a plane to fly out back to Talkeetna, twelve days after we had arrived.

We did it.

Once back in Talkeetna, Jason and Ryan go to the Park Rangers office and register our exit and successful summit. Then they both go and drop off our green buckets. Myself and Kaylee went to get a table for a celebratory breakfast in a local restaurant, filled with climbers.

CHAPTER 12
KOSCIUSZKO (KOSI)

Mount Kosciuszko or Kosi for short, is basically a walk to the summit.

Mount Kosciuszko is mainland Australia's highest mountain at 2,228 meters (7,310 ft) above sea level. It's located within the Kosciuszko National Park, and only a thirteen kilometer return walk to the summit from the ski town in Thredbo Village.

I say "walk" because it cannot really be considered a hike. There is a really nice path and a great summit rock at the top.

Mount Kosciuszko is on the Bass version of the 7 Summits list, therefore I had to do it. Carstensz on the other hand is on the Messner 7 Summit list.

Steve came with me and we combined it with a short visit to Australia. We had always talked about going to Australia together. I was still "strolling both sides of the line", as my psychiatrist had once put it, considering do I leave or do I continue to stay in this relationship, praying for clarity and direction. Regardless, we went together.

We first stopped in Sydney, took in the sites and explored the city. We then drove to Thredbo where we stayed a night in the ski village, so I could "climb" Kosciuszko.

Early on November 16, 2019, I got ready. I prepared my water bottle, snack, camera, phone, and my flags, and headed up the empty ski hill.

You can also take the chairlift, making the summit day even shorter but the lift didn't start operating until 8:30 am and I honestly wanted to hike/walk all of Kosciuszko. After all, it's the only peak in the 7 Summits series you can do within a few short hours, and without the need for acclimatization!

On my way to the Summit, I could see no one was on the peak. It felt great. It's not every day that you can have a summit peak to yourself or can complete a solo "climb" of one of the 7 Summits!

When I reached the top, I set-up my tripod, took selfies and then Facetimed my grandkids – Ethan and Julia. Again, it's not every day you can Facetime your grandkids from one of the 7 Summits.

Twenty minutes later, on my way down, Steve was coming up to do his own solo summit of Kosciuszko. Steve had taken the chairlift up and then, since he was there, decided to go to the Summit on his own as well.

This was my seventh summit. It didn't complete either 7 Summit lists though as both include Everest but it was "technically" my seventh summit. To avoid any contention that I completed the 7 Summits, I was doing both versions of the lists, and completing eight total summits. For the record though, Carstensz and Kosciuszko, the two mountains that differ on the lists, do not have any similarities!

With this one complete, it was on to Everest for my last Peak. At least everyone agrees about Everest.

CHAPTER 13
MIND OVER MOUNTAIN

*I had been scheduled to go to Everest in the Spring of 2020,
but Covid-19 happened and Everest closed,
just like the rest of the World.*

*But then it started opening in 2021 and my first attempt
to finished the 7 Summits, did not go well.*

After my attempt to summit Everest in the mid of the COVID-19 pandemic failed, in the Spring 2021, my financial advisor, insurance broker extraordinaire, and good friend Kim sent me a message because I was feeling defeated and sorry for myself. She asked me to consider that Everest was not the mountain I needed to climb, conquer, it was myself.

When I started training again for take two of Everest I realized she was right.

Take two was without Steve and was the end of more than a decade of feeling small. I don't mean short, as I am short, I mean small. Let me explain.

It had been twelve years, eight of barely living. I say barely living because living in a constant fog or like you are on a fast train waiting to derail at any moment is not living.

It was that fated day of April 7, 2009 when my life changed. I had come home from work with a migraine, and Steve hadn't been home, but when I looked inside the home office, on my way to my room, I saw his computer on. I walked over to look at what was on the screen and couldn't understand what I was reading:

Hi Carol,

Thank you for meeting me today. I was very nice. I enjoyed walking around with you and teasing you; and trying to kiss you!!! Until you finally gave in!!! I guess my persistence worked. You have very soft lips which I would like to explore again... I hope that you also liked kissing me --we were under a little bit of time pressure with you ready to run --one hand on the door--lol---but overall, we did pretty well!! I know I don't fit perfectly into what you are looking for in terms of "timing", but I hope that you will decide to overlook it and we can just try to make it work --I think that you will find that whatever we decide to do in the future, from kissing to if you decide to more --that you will be comfortable and secure with me -I'm a very attentive and gentle lover --from just nibbling on your ear to kissing your lips - I want us both to enjoy each other --that is important to me.

Anyways, I forgot to mention before you left that if you feel like calling to chat ---please do!!!

Jamie

ps --if you decide that you might want to continue in our path --as slow or fast as you wish - I want to take my ad down if it is ok with you and you think you want to pursue something with me.....I'm just looking to feel how I felt with you today while we were kissing -just with one person. Holding you, cuddling, kissing, touching a bit, and maybe one day we'll move on to more, but in a room type of thing....

bye again.."

My heart was pounding out of my chest. The email was sent from a Jamie to a Carol. Who was Jamie? Then I looked at the email box and on the left side panel, I saw folders labeled Amparo, Craig's List, Sarah, Trina and Various.

That was the day my world collapsed. I felt like a dump truck packed with rubble had crushed into me. I had started shaking and all I could do was reach for the phone and dial Steve's number. When he answered, I just blurted out:

"Who is Carol?"

I heard a thump as Steve dropped the phone. I called again and heard him pick up the line, but he stayed silent.

"Who is Carol and who is Jamie?". I had repeated over and over again.

"No one..." was all Steve answered me. He was driving home.

He had forgotten to close his computer when he took Daisy to the nearby dog park.

By the time Steve got home, I had read through enough emails to figured out that Jamie was Steve. After I hysterically screamed for a while, I made him delete the email account and then spent that whole night on the floor in the fetal position crying. He had been cheating on me with so many women. I was heartbroken, angry, and hurt. I was devastated.

A few days later, when I was a bit more composed, I recovered the email account from Yahoo. It was then that I learned Steve had been cheating on me for a very long time. There was some evidence back to 2006, but even more since 2008.

I learned that Steve, aka Jamie had accounts and ads in Ashley Madison, Adult Finder, and Lavalife. He also advertised in Kijiji's personal adds.

What disgusted me the most had been one of the ads he used on Craig's list to attract available women and the fact that the women that responded were willing to cheat on their partners as well. It read:

"......at least read my posting so you can understand why I'm looking for a special woman - a woman whose emotional and physical needs are not being met - possibly an ED issue or a circumstance like my own... .

I am a married man who has not been able to make love to my wife since she became disabled 2 years ago. While driving by herself, my wife was involved in a four-car collision and sustained a spinal cord injury - resulting in partial paralysis of her lower body (paraplegia). She is now in a wheelchair and in all likelihood will never be able to walk again.

Because I do still love my wife and choose to honor the commitment I made to her in marriage (in sickness AND in health), I have obviously decided to remain by her side. I hope to stay married to her forever but the truth is that the past years have been very difficult for me as well as for her. In addition to having the stress of being my wife's caretaker, I have also missed out on the two-way intimacy that my wife and I used to have regularly. We are still able to be affectionate with one another. After alot of time and thought, I finally came to the decision that I needed to do something to reclaim my own happiness - which had been lost since my wife's accident. I am searching for one woman who is open-minded and willing to be lovers - we would start as friends first. Hopefully there is one special woman out there who might be interested in such an arrangement. If you can understand my situation, you'll gain a great friend and lover who will make sure that you're happy with the time we spend together. I consider myself to be a very "giving" lover and I'm very affectionate too. This would be a discrete affair from both sides. Just so you know, I'm open to meeting a woman of any race and body type (from thin to curvy), and ages 25-50. I myself am white with an athletic body type, workout at a gym 3 times a week since I was a kid. I have a full head of blonde hair and clean shaven. Thank you for reading my post."

Kim knew all this, as I had confided in her. She had always been someone I could confide in over the years. I didn't have the courage to leave and I was unhappy, with suicidal thoughts many days. There were days driving to work that I would imagine dying if I drove my car really fast against a wall. Countless mornings I imagined just driving in front of the train, as I waited for it to pass on Winston Churchill Blvd.

After all this, I stayed. It was not yet my breaking point.

My breaking point came when Steve announced he was going to Mexico to get his face, chin, chest, and more done. He told me the week before I was schedule to leave for Everest in 2021. We fought about this trip. I rationalized that if plastic surgery was so important to him, he could get it done in Toronto, but he insisted on Mexico. I simply took that as him going with another woman, so I told him, "If you go to Mexico, we have no marriage left."

Steve, who was standing inside our walk-in closet, turned to me with such vengeance and disgust in his eyes, and simply answered , "do you think we have a fucking marriage?"

He left for Mexico and I left for Everest.

CHAPTER 14
EVEREST 2021

When I went to Everest in 2021, I was a walking Zombie.
I was empty. Scared. More than twenty two years
of my life were over.

Everest had been canceled the previous year because of Covid-19 and even though we were still in the midst of the pandemic, we were once again being allowed to travel, with all the restrictions. The North Side (Chinese side) remained closed, and that was the side I had originally intended to do and signed up for. I got convinced to do the South Side as we all thought it would be the year with less people. After all, we were still in a pandemic. Unfortunately, it became the year Nepal issued the most permits to hike Everest, ever. Even more than in 2019, where Nirmal "Nims" Purja's picture of the "traffic jam" of people making their way to the summit, made headlines around the world.

About a month after arriving, I left Everest.

Making the decision to leave was heart breaking, painful and one that I thought over very well. I cried a lot in my tent. And prayed. I cried as I wrote my original blog and Facebook post.

I didn't become the first Portuguese woman to have climbed the 7 Summits then, but I was ok. I was safe.

I had heard first-hand stories about trekking into Everest base camp. Some stood by the thought that if you can make it to base camp, through the Khumbu Valley, without getting sick, you were halfway to reaching the summit.

Well, my first symptoms started while having a hot chocolate in Namche during our trek to Everest base camp. The trek was intended to climb slowly and help our bodies acclimatize. But for me, it was the start of stomach problems I was unable to recuperate from.

Nine days of trekking proved to be taxing on my body. I was hit with intense diarrhea, vomiting and even after taking meds, I was not able to recuperate my strength. I became tired, dehydrated and even managed to humiliate myself days later, during a training session at base camp, next to the ice fall. At 53 years old, I soiled my pants. I was unable to control myself. I couldn't take off my harness in time. I have never been so embarrassed in my life, and yet I had to smile and pretend nothing happened. I bet that's not what you hear every day about climbing or see posted on Facebook.

Everest is not a normal mountain. It's the highest, but not the most beautiful in my opinion. At least not from the South Side (Nepal) side. You require a lot of technical climbing skills to navigate the ice fall for example.

Yes, there were fewer ladders and no section had three or more ladders tied together as you may have seen on YouTube. But even so, the route was very long from base camp to Camp 1. There were lots of vertical ice ascents and there were a lot of pitches that your average mountaineer may find very technical.

After a few delays, because of an earlier avalanche and the route being closed, on April 25 we were ready to move up to Camp 1. At 12:30 am we got up and were ready to walk by 2:00 am.

That day I thought my stomach was feeling better, but about thirty minutes later, by crampon point (location on the ice where our crampons need to go on), I needed to go the bathroom. It was a good place I thought, to get it over with, because no other place on the route would be available to go safely. Done. I was still feeling good.

After a few ascents, more climbing, more ascending, waiting in line, more ascending, we heard the firm voice of our lead guide who was up ahead, telling us to "duck". We looked up and saw a white powder cloud coming towards us, a serac falls. It collapsed into a crevasse thankfully, but I needed to go again to the bathroom!

I believe it was around this time that I lost sense of time and where I was. Against my guide's advice, I took my harness off and hid behind a rock, or it could have been a large block of ice. I could have fallen into a crevasse but all I was thinking at that moment, was that I needed to use the bathroom.

There were so many people on the ropes and path. People were no longer climbing and enjoying. Everyone was trying to get ahead, move, trying not to fall, and move ahead of the person in front of them. Here it was each for their own. Climbing the ice fall was the wild west, with a traffic jam of climbers, trying to prove they were tougher than the abyss of crevasses and slippery floors. Trying to race against the mountain. Fischer, the guide with me, kept asking if I was ok. He was worried about my bathroom breaks. After a while, I admitted I was suddenly cold, even though we had just finished a rope ascent. That was when he suggests that with my condition, we should turn back, while I had the strength to descend. I agreed.

He communicated with our lead guide Jacob via radio and that's what we did. Trying to descend when there was a caravan of people going up and only one rope was pretty hard. The route down is harder than going up. On many pitches Fischer was my human anchor. This demonstrated the high caliber of the mountain guides Mountain Trip employs. I felt safe but I was weak.

Back at base camp, I got into my tent and cried. I was letting everyone down.

On all the other mountains I had been able to feel Jesus push and pull me. I was able to sense him. Not this time. Even though I begged, I felt I was walking through a soulless place. Perhaps I was. Perhaps it was the souls of all the climbers that have died there and were never found.

The next morning my guides provided assurance and suggested we could go up the next morning and they would get a Sherpa to take my backpack so I could reserve my energy. Other climbers had taken advantage of it I was told the day before. I could still go to Camp 1 and meet the rest of the group. They told me I would not be very behind schedule.

But the 14 pounds I was carrying in my backpack was not the issue. My body was weak now after almost 20 days of passing gas, pain, cramps, diarrhea, feeling bloated, lack of energy, and being afraid to eat.

When I first told my family that I couldn't continue, I received words of encouragement to keep going. You are strong; you have trained for so long for this; you can do it, they said. We believe in you and we are proud of you they kept telling me even though I knew I had to stop.

Their words of encouragement only made me feel guiltier. I did not want to disappoint them or anyone – but I was beaten, and being on the ice fall felt cold, like a cave in the night, a tomb, and I did not want to die there. Not to mention, there was no bathroom!

I had started climbing the 7 Summits almost four years before and had completed seven of the eight summits, with Everest being the last remaining mountain to climb in both the Messner and Bass versions. I always enjoyed the climbs. I had summited all of them on my first attempt. Reaching the summit on each mountain had always been a bonus. The real win was that I had found myself in the mountains, through the climbs, and had enjoyed what the mountains had taught me so far.

This was different. I knew I did not have the strength to reach the summit and go through the icefall six times. I was only at our first rotation. That climbing season, crossing the icefall was taking some teams twenty hours to reach Camp 1. I did not have the strength at this point. Adding to the degree of danger on the icefall, where one needs to move as quickly as possible, my ailments increased the danger to myself, my guide and sherpa.

Climbing motivates you, pushes you. I of course, had been doing it only to raise awareness for mental health and end the stigma surrounding it, on behalf of Peaks for Change Foundation. The personal accomplishments just became part of the journey. They had never been the goal. The goal had been to raise funds for CAMH and the Bridging clinic, however we didn't raise as much as I had hoped.

Then, as I battled my body, willing it to cooperate so I could climb, I decided to listen. I acknowledged I couldn't continue to climb. It would have been hypocritical of me to keep going when my body was telling me it couldn't. Only my ego wanted to keep going but that could have, would have, put not only myself at risk but also my guides and sherpas. They would have done anything to ensure my safety. It was not fair for me to put them in that position.

So, putting aside my own insecurities, embarrassment, fears, demons, short comings and anxiety, I made the decision to stop.

It was not an easy decision. I had messaged Steve as I was trying to decide what to do, feeling defeated. I needed someone to tell me it was ok to go home. He simply messaged back and said that if I wanted to quit, to go ahead and do so.

That message was followed by another asking if I had contacted Kim about my insurance. I lied and said yes. Then he messaged back with a bombardment of questions, and said if the insurance covered the helicopter, the flight home, the fee I had paid Mountain Trip, etc, and if she told me in writing that was the case, to go ahead and quit.

I cried so much it was hard to breathe. I prayed and prayed to God to either let me die or show me what to do.

A few moments later, I got a message from Emmanuel. "Hey you! Your girls messaged me, what is going on?" he asked.

I messaged back and told him how sick I was, and what had been happening.

He responded, "Well sounds like turning around was the right decision. Rest. See how you feel in the morning. You feel like coming home. Come home."

I know he was just being supportive like Nicole and Patricia.

"Maybe in the morning you will say, 'fuck it, I am going to do this!'. Remember in Carstensz you got sick going up, on Summit day? What happens in Carstensz, stays in Carstensz :)," he continued.

"Emm, it has been Carstensz for like three weeks now, since I was hiking into BC," I messaged back.

"Ema, come home. The mountain will still be there another time," Emmanuel responded.

It was all I needed to hear. I just needed someone to understand how sick I had been feeling. I just needed someone to give me permission that is was ok to leave. I needed someone to tell me what to do.

"Ok," I messaged back and turned off my stat phone. After crying for what seemed hours, I went to tell our base camp manager and Fischer, my guide, I wanted a helicopter from base camp and I wanted to leave to Kathmandu and then return home. My expedition was over.

I didn't tell Steve until a few minutes before the helicopter was due for landing. I didn't want to fight anymore, listen to negativity, or have any more doubts planted in my mind. I was already packed. He was in Kathmandu, as he had planned on hiking to base camp and be there after I summited. He was recovering from his facelift, and I honestly did not want to see him. I hadn't understood why he still traveled to Nepal, as he had told me we had no marriage left.

When I arrived in Kathmandu he messaged me to ask what hotel I was staying at and that he would come to see me and we would have dinner. He spoke to me as if we had not been married for more than twenty two years, as if we were friends or something. I was broken, sick and tired and simply said, I couldn't see him because of Covid. I was going to stay in my room and wait for my Covid test, to see if I could fly home the next day. He agreed very fast so I assumed he was as relieved not to see me, as I was not to see him. Then he said he was leaving in the morning to start his base camp hike.

And that was that. I made my way home the following day. It was the end of my Everest attempt and the official end of my marriage.

I have to admit, the icefall frighted me to the bones. I want to believe my stomach problems were Jesus's way of telling me I was not meant to climb Everest, that time around. It was His way of keeping me safe, because once I decided to go home, a warm feeling washed over me. I felt my lungs expand and they filled with air.

Once home, I quarantined for fourteen days as mandated by the government. All my Covid-19 tests had been negative.

I felt tired for weeks after. Sleeping came easily during the day, as if my body wanted to shut off my brain as it drifted to "what if's". Being in quarantine, not being able to leave the house, took a toll on my self-esteem and mental health. I felt like a criminal.

After I consulted with my family doctor, the question was raised if I had been suffering from altitude sickness and no one caught it. I will never know. What I can tell you is my stomach still hurt for weeks after when I would eat.

After I left Everest, one other team member was evacuated from Camp 2 because of altitude sickness. He returned home to the US.

It was reported that Nepal issued 408 climbing permits that season, which was a record high number of permits since permits have been issued to climb Everest. I believe that my getting sick was a blessing.

We had opted to climb the South Side because that season originally promised to be one of the lowest number of people climbing and would afford us the luxury of enjoying the mountain. Crowds in 2019 had led to fatalities; crowds seen in that now famous photo of hundreds of climbers lined up to summit – all on oxygen. The year of my first attempt had promised to be more of the same.

Climbing mountains, or even hills, is therapeutic and liberating. It does wonders for your mental health and is great exercise. Reaching the summit of any peak is breath-taking. The views afforded will be forever etched in my mind. But climbing to reach the summit in a line-up "around the block" loses its appeal, its purpose. In my humble opinion. After so much waiting in line, when you reach the top, would you think it was worth it? I know that when I climbed Elbrus in Russia, the high winds and crowds made it anti-climactic for me. I barely had time to take a photo when I had to leave the summit space.

For a few months after, people encouraged me to try again next season. I only smiled. Secretly inside me, I never wanted to go back. But then the "what if" demons started to torture me.

CHAPTER 15
EVEREST, TAKE TWO

On Friday May 13, 2022 I summited Everest and finished what I started back in September 2017.

I arrived in Kathmandu on April 25, 2022. I still had to climb on the South Side, via Nepal, as China continued to have Everest closed to foreigners. This time I had decided to go with Furtenbach Adventures and did the Flash ascent. It's "Flash" because it's a rapid ascent version of climbing Everest; three weeks versus the standard two month expedition. I started my acclimatization at home using a hypoxic tent to sleep every night for eight weeks leading up to my departure to Nepal.

l made the conscious decision not to trek into base camp this time. That had been my determent last season. This cut the amount of time I would spend on the mountain. And, there was no need to go up and down the mountain to acclimatize and cross the dangerous ice fall.

The other factor for choosing Furtenbach Adventures was the unlimited oxygen available. Last season, even though I ended up not using it, when I counted the bottles in base camp and did the math, there would not have been enough for all of us to use freely. Furtenbach also mandates that all the Sherpas have oxygen, like the clients.

After waiting for the rest of the team to arrive the following day, we headed out the morning of April 27. Quite honestly, it felt good to leave Kathmandu. It was so dirty there and filled with so many people. The same as it was the previous year.

It felt a bit like déjà vu heading out, except this time the majority of our team spoke German. My teammates were primarily from Austria. Other than me, there were three others that spoke English as our primary language: an American writer, an older British gentleman, and a guy from Israel. There was one other female on the team, Cosima. Dr Cosima Eggenberger-Huspenina, also from Austria.

The others were supergiant German climbers who looked me over, trying to gauge if I belonged in their expedition. I felt a little self-conscious, but I took a deep breath and shrugged it off. I knew I belonged! I could do exactly what they could, I could climb. I was used to stares because I am short. I had lived with that for fifty-five years at that point. I knew some people were quick to judge based on appearances, and I didn't care.

We flew by helicopter, several helicopters actually as we were a big group, and landed in Kote. I didn't feel the dread of last year. This side of the Khumbu, a region in Nepal, was very different. I knew I could do this.

I kept focusing on repeating over and over, I can do it. I knew I had it this time. While we waited for our rooms in the lodge where we were spending the night, myself and Cosima went for a small walk nearby. We hiked towards a bridge over raging waters. The remoteness of this village, set in a valley surrounded by mountains reminded me of Carstensz and our trek in. I thought it was an omen, a good luck omen. The memory of Emmanuel calling me Jane of the jungle as I crossed over a similar bridge, brought an instant smile, and followed by a longing. For a moment I wished he was there.

After lunch we went for a small walk and I felt good, not out of breath, not tired and I was keeping pace better than some. This helped my self-confidence a little. When we got back to the village, we had tea and cookies inside the warm dining room of the Lama Lodge.

Heat in accommodations typically comes from yak poop, which smells bad since, you guessed it, it's burning poop! At the Lama Lodge however, the room was heated with real wood! It was a treat! That said, the accommodation itself was as bad as the lodges I remembered from last year. We waited for dinner, then headed to our cold room, where we crawled into a sleeping bag and hoped for sleep.

On April 28, day three of our expedition, I was glad to be moving along. Never thought I would say this, but I preferred a tent over the tea houses. Cosima was not feeling well, and said she had some stomach issues she thought might be bacteria. She's a doctor so I assumed she knew what she was talking about.

The older gentleman, who I learned was 68 years old, Graham was doing the signature climb expedition which meant he had his own guide and three sherpas, was also not feeling well. He had altitude affects. His head was hurting a lot. I was feeling pretty good even though I was not taking Diamox this time. Lukas had told me I would have to stop taking it at base camp anyways, so instead, I kept an eye on my hands for swelling as we completed our trek for the day.

The pace that day was relatively easy, and I wasn't short of breath. I enjoyed the hike more than I did last year and even took the opportunity to enjoy the beautiful scenery as we went.

As I moved along, I tried to keep my mind occupied, trying to think of only positive things. A few times I "wrote" fantasies in my mind! They made me smile and kept me moving with an extra step! I "wrote" several novels climbing the other mountains and this was no different. Occupying my mind helped distract me during the long days, and on this particular day, it allowed me to ignore all the German being spoken.

After dinner we had a lecture on altitude sickness and what we should and shouldn't be feeling.

The food was sparse at the tea house. There was no meat, and today there was no bread despite my having requested toast for the morning.

We spent day 4 of our expedition hiking. We made it to Khali, around lunch time, which was the last village before we went to climb Mera Peak. The term village was used loosely since there were only a few buildings including accommodations for tourists. This village was considered base camp for Mera Peak.

I still felt good and enjoyed pushing myself to keep up with the pace, which was awesome. This year I didn't find myself tired or struggling.

There were more people here, getting ready to go to the top of Mera Peak. There was a group of Greeks that stimulated thoughts of Covid-19, causing us some jitters, not to mention it was freaking cold as well.

After lunch, we did an acclimatization climb of the moraine. It was high. It had a 500 m height increase achieved by walking on a thin path. Every so often, out of the corner of my eye, I could see how high we were and I panicked a little, but then talked myself down and continued climbing.

A few climbers did not go up, like Cosima. I don't understand why, but nevertheless to those of us that went, Lukas said at the top that he was really excited how well we all were doing. He said the pace was great and we all seemed to be acclimatizing well.

I did feel good though I continued to be a little nervous that I was not taking my Diamox. I kept monitoring my liquid intake and output and kept looking at my hands for swelling. It was only day 4 but I was already tired of ginger lemon tea, so I switched to mint tea. Due to my fears of repeating last years' "shit happens", I was staying away from coffee.

As the day went on, the guys started talking to me more. They spoke English (with an accent). One climber in our group played trombone for the Vienna State Opera House. Believe it or not, he carried it with him and that day at our first break, he played for a few minutes!

The rest of the group's equipment (and we had lots) went to base camp with our duffels. There was more than usual because Red Bull was filming a documentary of our climb. In fact, one of the cameramen/producers came with us that day. His name was Philip. He spent most of his time with Lukas, taking stock footage on his own.

The next day, day 5, was a miserable day. We did an acclimatization hike on to Mera Peak and came back to sleep at the lodge. We went up to 5500 meters (18,044 feet), and then came down. This was a substitution to the rotations on Everest over the icefall, so I did not complain. However, we got hit with a lot of snow and got totally wet. We had to put all our clothes and backpacks around the wood stove to dry. The dining room of the lodge looked like a camping site, even with clothes lines.

To that point we had been without wi-fi and it was causing a morale problem. To top it off, every battery died here. My own stat phone battery had died as well. I had decided I would only recharge it once we reach Everest base camp since they charged $10 USD to charge each device there.

During our acclimatization hike we were roped in and I felt I did ok. The pace of the guides was ok but man, it was cold when we came down!

I became anxious to get this part done and just go to base camp and summit. It was cold! I can't emphasize that enough.

We hardly carried anything in our backpacks. We had porters to carry our boots and crampons to crampon point. This was helpful because there was almost two hours of climbing over rocks. It was slippery.

The following day, which was day 6 of our expedition, we climbed to Camp 1 of Mera Peak. The porters again took our expedition boots and crampons to crampon point. The plan had been, once we had summited Mera Peak, the porters would again be at crampon point, Wednesday morning, with our regular hiking boots, and we would exchange our footwear again before descending back to the village.

I hadn't felt I was too quick putting the boots and crampons on but seems I was, so I was put on the rope team that is faster. The guide was good, and his pace was awesome. I found it was such a difference from the previous year, when Jacob was always hiking so fast, hardly anyone could keep up. Sometimes I thought he enjoyed making everyone feel bad. I recalled Scott commenting on it as well.

A couple of guys were not very happy with me being on their rope, but tough luck for them. This time around, I had resigned myself not to care about what others thought or felt. I had come back, at great financial cost, to finish the seven summits, but more importantly, to prove to myself I could do it.

This time I wanted to just get it done.

Even though Cosima was climbing Mera Peak with us, she would then be climbing Lhotse. This meant I would be the only female in the Everest team after Everest base camp. Some of the men in our team irritated me quite a bit. How could they have such egos when some didn't even know how to walk on a roped line within a group! I think I was a bit irritated as well because they were always speaking German.

My tent was quite big. It seemed like a four person tent for two people which was nice. At Camp 1 we were at 18,612 ft (5,672 m).

The next day we moved up to the higher camp and it was tiring. This camp sat at 19,643 ft (6,000 m). It was a long, both hot and cold climb. But that's how climbing high mountains is. One minute the sun is blaring down on you, and the next there is a snowstorm.

After we reached camp, we rested for an hour and then went for another acclimatization hike up to 20,344 ft (6,200 m).

Comfort when climbing is not the highlight of an expedition, in reality it sucks. Being inside and sleeping in a cold tent and then having to go outside to pee is not luxury for sure.

At this high altitude and because we were moving fast, there was no kitchen tent. Instead, the Sherpas brought our food to our tents. Food consisted of whatever could be made using boiled water.

On day eight, I felt exhausted and I thought to myself, "Fuck". It was already eight days. It was no wonder tears started more easily! I missed my daughters, Ethan and Julia and home!

It was summit day for Mera Peak. And like I had gotten accustomed, God graced the top of mountain with sunshine, even though a short time before it seemed the weather would be horrible.

Mera Peak is not an easy mountain, standing at about 21,800 feet (6,476 m). It did however afford a great view from the top though! Mera Peak is similar in height to Camp 2 on Everest and was the reason we climbed it. This climb replaced a rotation on Everest. It was worth it.

The summit push was a steep climb, with only 3 ropes that lead right to the summit. I was happy to realized I still remembered how to use a jumar! The whole group summited.

It had been hard to sleep during the night as it was so freaking cold on this mountain, maybe because it's so exposed. But I managed and had enough energy to summit with the group.

There were also lots of crevasses to jump over; one that was particularly scary. Little did I know at the time, this was a walk in the park. My heart felt it would get stuck on my throat as I jumped over it.

On day nine the plan had been to leave Mera Peak and head to Everest base camp. Our wakeup call was at 2:30 am, and I had slept horribly because of the cold. Our team was to be ready to head out at 4:00 am. We had been warned that if we were not ready at 4:00 am with crampons on, we would not go down until a Sherpa could take us, so we made sure to be ready. I was anxious to be on the helicopters that would take us to Everest base camp but first, we needed to get back to the lodge to catch them.

This time around, arriving at Everest base camp was nice. In a weird way, it felt good to be returning. Furtenbach's camp was also a step up from my camp last year in terms of comfort, but the ice fall was 45 minutes away to crampon point. My default was to let it feel daunting, but I mindfully pushed those negative thoughts to the back of my mind.

As we arrived, a couple people were leaving. Diarmund, a familiar face from last year had gotten sick and was leaving. Diarmund had trekked in. I was disappointed he was leaving as he spoke English and I had forged a friendship with him last year. He was a recognizable face on the mountain for me, but unfortunately he was leaving. There was another female leaving as well. She had been sick and couldn't handle the cold.

Seeing these people leave shook me up. I cried with fear. I was scared again. I kept thinking that darn ice fall wanted to beat me.

I was able to speak briefly to Diarmund, and he gave me his internet code and password. He had purchased unlimited access for $250 USD and since he was leaving, he gave it to me. Internet provided a much needed means of connection for me, especially since Lukas had told us to remain in our camp and not visit others. In reality, I didn't have anyone to visit anyways. I did know Marta, a teammate from last year who was climbing with "Nims", and could see their camp from ours but I didn't feel the need to visit.

The Red Bull TV crew was all there. They had been taking footage while we climbed Mera Peak. Philip would be the only member of the film crew that would go to the summit of Everest with us. I have to admit that having the film crew there took my mind off my fear. It provided a great distraction.

By day ten it felt like an eternity since day one. So many things to remember, so many things to keep an eye on. While we all practiced our ice work that afternoon, I kept reminding myself to breathe and go slow. I knew how to ice climb, to use my Jumar, but I had to focus to remember the figure 8 sequence we needed to use.

At this point my eyes were swelling a bit. I considered taking Diamox the following day. I paid attention to my pee to see if I was drinking enough and used my pee bottle to determine my hydration levels. I found I was definitely not drinking enough so I worked to change that.

That morning I had finally figured out the satellite phone and heard my kid's voices. I was so happy. That small thing brought me so much joy and comfort. Even though we were supposed to have internet, it didn't work. It felt like déjà vu from the previous year.

Day eleven was cloudy, which meant it was COLD! That didn't stop us from training. After breakfast, we practiced the ropes, using our jumar, climbing on a ladder and of course belaying down with the figure 8.

Upon return from our training session the Internet was finally up. This thing we take for granted back home was finally available to us here. I was so thankful to Diarmund for giving me his access that I sought out his Facebook and saw the post he wrote about having to make the decision to leave. I knew that feeling from last year and my heart went out to him.

In the afternoon, we practiced using our oxygen. The oxygen bottle I would have to carry was 3.2 kg, with my spares being carried by one of my Sherpas, along with an extra regulator and mask for me. We were using a continuous flow system and were encouraged to start using it at Camp 2. I was in!!!!

The camera crew taped our oxygen practice session in our rec room dome tent. I call it a rec room because we had blow-up couches, games, a tv with movies to watch, coffee and hot water for tea readily available, and it was heated.

Lukas made a presentation in English and we all tried our systems. With the film crew there I was glad I had combed my hair before this training session.

Lukas talked about the incident on the north side of Everest in 2018 when all the regulators stopped working. The company that supplied our oxygen and regulators, Summit Oxygen, was the same company involved in this incident. We were assured the problem had been fixed.

We were also told we could use as much oxygen as we want, but that we needed to start at a slow flow rate. To put this into perspective, at the summit, near the 20 meters of Hillary Steps, we could be cranking the flow to 8. At camp when we slept, we adjusted our flow rate to 0.5.

When we finished training for the day, Lukas broke the news that the weather window was early. He said that due to a phenomena scientists say never happened and because of whatever was happening in India at the time, the weather in the Himalayas was expected as high as -17 Celsius on the top of Everest. This was the same temperature we had at Mera Peak.

This meant our summit push would happen in a couple of days! I didn't know what to think or say. I couldn't tell if I was scared, ready or excited…or just plain scared.

On Everest, it's tradition to participate in the Puja Ceremony before leaving base camp and beginning the journey to the summit. Climbers and Sherpa take part in the Puja Ceremony. It's a literal "rite of passage". The Puja Ceremony is performed to make contact with divine Sagamartha, Mount Everest, and pray for a safe expedition.

In preparation for the ceremony, a large cairn is constructed with long strands of prayer flags. The team makes an offering of special foods and drinks; and brings their climbing gear to be blessed for the journey.

Our Puja Ceremony occurred on day 12 of the expedition.

I had wrestled in 2021 with worshiping a Buddhist idol. I am Christian. I worship my Father, God, through his son Jesus Christ. Not Idols. This time on Everest I had an army praying for me back home; Pastor Sam and the prayer team of Village Church, Toronto West, were on it, advocating for me with Jesus. My friend Julia prayed and I prayed. I was respectful, being present at the ceremony, but I did not take any food, drink, and I declined to have the traditional sandalwood power mark my face. I also did not put my ice axe or crampons, helmet or harness to be blessed. Jesus would be with me, and only he would protect me.

After lunch Lukas made it official, we were leaving base camp at midnight the following day which technically was Monday. We were aiming to go for the Summit, Friday the 13th. We were all asked not to post it on social media, since we had such a big group plus the TV crew. He didn't want other groups to know when we were planning to go. The weather window was anticipated to be ten days long.

Later that day we met with our Sherpas in preparation. One of mine had summited Everest nine times; four times from the North side and five from the South. His name was Nima Sherpa. The other was a quiet man that I didn't get to talk with much.

We had to be ready with all our gear for our Sherpas after breakfast the next day. This included the food we would need for the upper camps. I had chosen vegan, lactose free breakfast food to minimize any stomach problems, and jellybeans!

As the day wore on, I continued to drink a lot of water (of course). I was nervous but also strangely calm. This was really happening!

Day thirteen of the expedition, from the day I had landed in Kathmandu, it was Mother's Day and I missed the girls dearly. I cried.

After breakfast, Lukas gave us letters from our families. Furtenbach had asked our families for letters, without us knowing. I read letters from Nicole, Nicolas and Patricia. I read Julia's and Ethan's on WhatsApp. I missed them so much. I talked to them on the phone and told them of our plans of moving up at midnight.

Then I messaged Emmanuel and he called me. I was crying. He asked me if I was ok and I told him I was just missing the girls. I updated him on our plans to move from base camp and he knew that the ice fall was what scared the shit out of me. Then, as a true friend says, "You got this. The icefall is just a moving river, that very few people have the chance to walk on. Ok?"

As he said those words to me, from Canada, I was looking out the tent at the ice fall. As tears rolled down from my eyes, I shook my head in agreement, as if he could see me. But he couldn't.

He asked, "did you hear me?" Then I remembered I had to talk. "Yeah, Ok," I responded with salty tears reaching my lips.

This was it. I needed to do this. I needed to do it for me, my girls and grandkids, but I also wanted to do it for Emmanuel. I needed him to be proud of me because he believed in me unconditionally.

Shortly after, the Sherpas came to pick up my gear to carry up. Hours later, after just resting laying down, anxious, it was time. We left for the ice fall.

The next few days were a blur.

But climbing over the icefall was not as scary as it had been last year. I did not feel the coldness, darkness, or dread. The ladders weren't as scary as they once seemed, and I did great I had to admit.

My climbing Sherpa, Nima was wonderful and never left my side. I was even able to enjoy the beauty of the huge seracs but moved fast when Nima said so, because of the danger of them falling on us.

The crevasses were the scariest thing I had to deal with. My anxiety levels doubled at the sight of each one; and there were so many. Both Nima and one of the guides help me at each one. I have short legs and some of the crevasses were huge. I kept telling myself the Sherpas jumped over them all day, but at the site of each one, my heart raced uncontrollably. I was thankful our lead guides didn't disappear as they had last year. This time was a totally different climb.

We got to Camp 1, then the next day Camp 2. The following day, we got to Camp Three, which sits on a 30-degree snow slope with rocky exposed ledges on which our tents were perched. The view is great, but you need to watch every step when you leave the tent to poo. Pee? Well, you do that in your pee bottle.

Then, with full oxygen flowing in our masks, early morning Thursday, we made our way to the South Col, which is Camp 4.

Making our way up to the South Col was not easy. It was Everest I know, but it was a long way up. And the heat was at times unbearable. Yes, the heat! The sun shining down on us at such high altitude, when we were wearing a down full body suit was not the most comfortable thing. But you couldn't be fooled to take it off because flash freezing temperatures could happen without warning, at any moment. Just one small cloud teasingly passing in front of the sun could change everything.

We climbed up, and up and up.

When we arrived, we quickly realized it was not your regular camp. It was windy. There were oxygen bottles everywhere. Ours were stacked neatly and formed a nice pyramid pile. Lukas had said we had 30% more oxygen than needed, and it was visibly true.

There was also more garbage in the camp than in all the previous ones below.

Actually, there were pieces of broken tents everywhere. No doubt the constant high winds were the culprit but it could also be the cold and the fact that without proper oxygen, one is a little hypoxic. Combine that with the fact that some people don't pick up after themselves, it's a perfect storm for the messy scene that surrounded us.

It's colder there and as soon as you took your oxygen mask off, your breathing was labored. The South Col is only used as a resting place for what is smack in front of you... Everest. It sits in the middle of Everest and Lotse, at 26,300 feet.

Last year I had been unimpressed with Everest. I felt no joy, I was sick and I was battling my mind. But on this journey, the sheer height of Everest from the South Col was pretty humbling.

We could see people coming down, although some may have been going up, it was hard to tell. Our group was told to go rest and get ready to start at 8:00 pm with our Sherpa.

On time at 8:00 pm we headed out. Nima was in front of me, and another Sherpa behind with a backpack full of oxygen. There were already many lights on the face of the mountain. On each mountain they always reminded me of fireflies. These tiny lights, seemed to move slowly, far away.

Surprisingly we very quickly reached them. We could only see climber silhouettes illuminated by their headlights. They seemed to be going very slow. And then slower. At first, I welcomed the pace, as it allowed me to go slower, but soon it became annoying. I could feel Nima getting impatient as well.

We overtook three groups, but then came to a place we could no longer overtake anyone. The lineup was huge! We moved slower and slower. I watched people in front of me struggle at every rope transfer point with their carabiners. I found myself judging their equipment, judging their speed, and silently felt annoyed at what I perceived were amateurs.

This was one of the problems in Everest. It's a huge money maker for the government of Nepal. Many companies, expedition operators, take on clients / climbers that have insufficient experience climbing, proper protocols and etiquette. This was one of the reasons for bottlenecks like in the famous 2019 picture taken by Nims that circulated around the world, showing climbers lined up on the ridge. If one or two climbers stop and don't move, in some sections there is no space for anyone to pass them

We climbed and climbed and climbed. At night you could only focus on your feet, and I did, I felt good. Nima changed my oxygen bottle at some point.

We passed a man sitting on the left of the ridge we were climbing. He seemed exhausted, his face freezing and next to him was what I assumed to be his Sherpa, sitting with no expression. The man did not have an oxygen mask on and it haunted me. Nima just turned back and told me to keep moving. I'm sure it haunted him too.

What seemed like shortly after, I looked to the side and saw the golden glow of the sun rising. Shortly after, Nima pointed it out to me. "Sunrise" he said and pointed. I just nodded my head in acknowledgement.

I started to see and as I glanced around me, I knew we were really high. My anxiety started to form.

Then just like that, we were at the Hillary Step. Which is not a step at all. The Step is named after Sir Edmund Hillary. After the earthquake of 2015 the original rock face got destroyed and even though it is no longer the original 40 feet (12 m) in height, it is still really scary.

Climbing the Hillary Step had the danger of a 10,000 ft (3,000 m) drop on one side and a 2,400 meter (8,000 ft) drop on the other. Or in rock climbing terms, it was rated a class 4 rock climb. Now all that is left is a couple of slanted, slippery rocks, that have a web of ropes for how you are supposed to cross and keep yourself attached to the mountain. When you look down, you see the abyss.

My heart raced. I asked Nima to increase my oxygen. I don't know if he did or just pretended since he had been saying he was increasing on occasions in the lower camp and never did.

Then I saw it. I froze. It was a dead body. Just there, at the bottom of the second step. He still had his crampons on, laying on his back with his goggles on and everything, as if he just laid down to take a rest. He even had his oxygen mask on his face.

The down on the left side of his suit shoulder was showing, as some people had been using this shoulder as a stepping-stone. It was only then that I realized he was dead and I panicked.

OMG. He was dead. I couldn't take my eyes off him. It was hard to grab the ropes, as there was really nowhere to put your feet. My boots and crampons slipped easily as I tried to stay far away from the body. I managed to climb on top of the step and get passed that section. It was not what you were supposed to do, but let's be realistic, at that spot, you either freeze, and not make it, or you try to move how you can.

Fear filled my soul. What was I doing there? Why was I there? Nima told me to move, and I did as I was told mechanically, but I was silently talking, begging Jesus to please keep me safe and not let me die. I had never been so afraid for my life.

Then we reached the summit. Just like that.

I sat. I pretended to be happy, but I was shaking inside, and I didn't want to look around. Nima took my photos and was excited to be there. He took videos and made me get up and look around. It was his 10th time standing there. I just wanted to leave. But we took a few pictures together and Nima was very excited to point out Manaslu, his hometown, to me. Manaslu is the eighth highest mountain in the world.

We got ready to leave the summit and, on the way back down we stopped in our tracks. We couldn't go anywhere. There was a line of people on the ridge, just coming and coming. There was no end. Their expressions seemed to be one of anger, or maybe they were just as scared as I was.

We had our safety carabiner on the line and just stood there waiting, as people passed us, moved around us. We stood there for what seemed like hours. I started to worry about my oxygen. I imagined dying there and again I silently begged God to spare my life. I reprimanded myself on the stupidity of being there. Tears streamed from my eyes, then I stopped myself as I knew I couldn't take my goggles off, because my eyelids could freeze.

Then there was a break and Nima told me we needed to go. I moved fast, but then we were at the Hillary Step again, and I panicked. I couldn't climb over the step this time, as there were others doing that. I didn't want to touch the dead body but Nima assured me, rather sternly, that I could do it and that I should watch him. He doubled our safety with a second carabiner on the ropes that wrapped around of what is left of the step. He told me to do what he did, which was to lean back and just walk on the rock, trusting that the safety rope and the double carabiners would hold me. I took a deep breath, and did as he said, and it worked.

Somehow, we had lost the second Sherpa with the oxygen I noticed. Another Sherpa from our group crossed us and told Nima where the oxygen bottles were. Just before the end of the ridge, we made a short stop and Nima exchanged my oxygen bottle for another one before we continued to journey down.

I didn't want to climb anymore. Once we reach the South Col, I could hardly move I was so tired. Upon reaching the South Col, I could hardly move I was so tired. I was cold, physically spent and breathing from a new oxygen tank for the descent down. I couldn't help but think of the parallels in my own life. It served to remind me that I never allowed the proverbial "glass ceiling" or "limiting beliefs" hold me back. As tired as I was, as emotional as this day had been, I knew I had more to do before this venture was done.

Nima told me to rest for an hour, but not to sleep as we needed to descend to Camp 2. He helped me pack my sleeping bag. My whole body hurt.

I had been awake for more than 24 hours at that point and we still needed to descend to Camp 2. It took another six hours before we finally arrived at Camp 2. My ribs were killing me from so much belaying. Each belay I felt like my lungs were being crushed. Tears rolled down my cheeks a few times. I couldn't believe we had climbed that far up. How was it possible I kept asking myself.

I barely knew my name at that point. When we finally reached Camp 2, we were told that wake up the next morning was at 4:00 am so that we could get to the icefall while it was still cold. Awesome I thought sarcastically.

Something was dead inside me. I kept thinking of the body lying on the step. I later learned, even though there were a couple of slightly different versions of the story, what had happened. In essence, the version I want to hold on to, was that the body was an East Indian gentleman who lived in the United States. He and his wife had been climbing in 2019 when his wife's oxygen ran out and she fell to her death. He just laid there heart broken, with no will to survive.

We left Camp 2 on schedule at 4:00 am, whizzed by Camp 1 and we were back at the icefall making our way down.

We descended, belay after belay. I questioned myself several times, how many more belays; how high did I climb? I kept asking Nima how much further, and he gave me the same answer over and over again, "About ten more."

Hours later we were out of the icefall and reached the crampon point where we could finally take off our crampons. I hand them to Nima and told him to keep them. I wasn't going to be climbing anymore.

I also told him he could keep my down suit that he was carrying in his backpack as well. He smiled and thanked me. The down suit was a men's size small. To date, outdoor clothing companies still don't make a female version because I guess the market share is too small.

My suit had been generously given to me by RAB for my initial scheduled 2020 climb, before Covid-19 shut the world down. I was grateful for RAB's support and thought it was great to pass it on to someone that needed it. Nima needed a new down suit.

I was done.

I finished what I started. Four and a half years later, I had summited the 7 summits, both Messner's and Bass's versions. Eight mountains.

WHAT'S NEXT

"Ecotherapy is great for the mind."
~ Adam Beauchamp

When people ask me what's next, I tell them I am happy being at home.

But truth is, I miss training for a goal. I miss having an oriented purpose. It's affecting my mental health to be honest.

I once heard or read somewhere that climbing mountains is addictive. Well, they are. They affected me in ways I never imagined.

This four and a half year journey saved my life. It made me stronger and more resilient. I also found and experienced the presence, love and patience of God, in my soul.

So, what's next? I am thinking of starting a new puzzle; a new journey yet to unfold.

Acknowledgements

Gratitude to Jade Stevens for creating my book covers, website, etc,.

Gratitude for Carol McFarlane for her insight, great editing skills and thoughtfulness, which without, this book may have been a little harder to follow.

Gratitude to Tyler Stone, for training me, and letting me cry many times during our workouts, just because working out was better that wallowing in my sorrow from my broken heart. He kept me focused and helped me get some muscles.

Thank you to all the Peaks for Change Foundation Board Members for indulging me and supporting our believe and desire in ending the stigma of Mental Health.

Thank you for my new church family at Village Church in Toronto, for the prayer sessions as I climbed Everest, Take Two. Blessed.

Citations

Amanda MacMillan from Health.com, August 2, 2011
http://www.cnn.com/2011/HEALTH/08/02/sexual.assault.domestic.violence/index.html

Stop Violence Against Woman Org
https://www.stopvaw.org

Canadian Women's Foundation
https://canadianwomen.org

Secretariat of the Antarctica Treaty, Waste Management
https://www.ats.aq/e/waste.html

Copyright.
© Ema de Jesus Joao Bras Dantas

www.ingramcontent.com/pod-product-compliance
Lightning Source LLC
Chambersburg PA
CBHW070938180426
43192CB00039B/2338